SARA L. WESTON

Railroad Rebels: The Women Who Refused To Settle

To those brave women and girls who refused to settle, built communities within the railroad communities and forged a path to a life the helped them embrace adventure, danger, fun, pain, passion and authenticity.

Contents

Preface

Within the sinews of American history, straddling the line between myth and matter, a lesser-known tale of audacity courses through. It's the story of indomitable spirits, not just any spirits, but specifically those of women and girls who seized the steel veins crisscrossing the vast, rough-hewn terrains— the railways—to etch out a narrative of their own during the harshest of times: the Great Depression. This period bore witness to the birth and blossoming of a subculture that would leave indelible marks on the fabric of society: the hobo culture.

1

Chapter 1

The Origins of Train Hopping

1.1 Early Pioneers: Women on the Rails

Throughout history, there have been remarkable women who defied societal norms and embarked on daring adventures, choosing to live itinerant lives and ride the rails. These early pioneers of train hopping paved the way for future generations of women seeking freedom and independence. Their stories are a testament to the resilience, courage, and determination of women who dared to challenge the status quo.

1.1.1 Boxcar Bertha Thompson: The Legendary Train Hopper

One of the most legendary women train hoppers of all time is Boxcar Bertha Thompson. Born in 1894, Bertha Thompson grew up in a time when women were expected to conform to traditional roles. However, she had a burning desire for adventure and a yearning to break free from societal constraints.

Bertha's journey as a train hopper began during the Great Depression when she found herself homeless and destitute. She discovered that riding the rails offered a sense of freedom and a chance to escape the hardships of her everyday life. Bertha became known for her fearless spirit and her ability to navigate the treacherous world of train hopping.

1.1.2 Hobo Lobo: A Woman's Journey through the Great Depression

Another notable woman train hopper during the Great Depression was Hobo Lobo. Born as Mary Ellen Wilson in 1900, she adopted the name Hobo Lobo as she embraced the nomadic lifestyle of a hobo. Hobo Lobo traveled across the country, hopping from one train to another, in search of work and a better life.

Hobo Lobo's story is a testament to the resilience and resourcefulness of women during a time of great hardship. She faced numerous challenges, including harsh weather conditions, dangerous encounters, and the constant threat of arrest. Despite these obstacles, Hobo Lobo found solace and a sense of belonging within the tight-knit community of train hoppers.

1.1.3 Mona Bell: Riding the Rails in the Wild West

In the Wild West, where lawlessness and adventure reigned, Mona Bell emerged as a fearless woman train hopper. Born in the late 1800s, Mona Bell defied societal expectations and embarked on a life of adventure, riding the rails across the vast landscapes of the American West.

Mona Bell's story is one of resilience and determination. She faced the challenges of a harsh environment, including extreme weather conditions and the constant threat of danger. Yet, she found a sense of freedom and independence on the rails, forging her own path in a world dominated by men.

1.1.4 Steam Train Maury: A Trailblazer in the 20th Century

As the 20th century dawned, a new generation of women train hoppers emerged, including Steam Train Maury. Born in the early 1900s, Steam Train Maury defied societal expectations and embarked on a life of adventure, riding the rails across the United States.

Steam Train Maury's story is one of courage and determination. She faced the challenges of a rapidly changing world, navigating the evolving railroad system and adapting to new technologies. Despite the risks and dangers, Steam Train Maury found a sense of freedom and empowerment on the rails, inspiring other women to follow in her footsteps.

1.1.5 Colleen Anderson: Escaping the Constraints of Society

Colleen Anderson is another notable woman who chose to defy societal norms and embrace the nomadic lifestyle of a train hopper. Born in the mid-20th century, Colleen Anderson sought to escape the constraints of a conventional life and find her own path.

Colleen's story is one of self-discovery and empowerment. She found solace and freedom on the rails, forging connections with fellow train hoppers and embracing the camaraderie of the community. Colleen's journey serves as an inspiration to women who yearn for independence and adventure.

1.1.6 Hobo Girl Petula Williams: A Modern-Day Nomad

In more recent times, Hobo Girl Petula Williams has become a symbol of the modern-day nomad. Born in the late 20th century, Petula Williams chose to live a life of freedom and adventure, riding the rails and embracing the challenges and rewards of train hopping.

Petula's story is one of resilience and determination. She navigates the complexities of the modern railroad system, using her knowledge and experience to travel safely and responsibly. Petula's journey serves as a reminder that the spirit of train hopping lives on, inspiring a new generation of women to embrace a life of adventure and independence.

These women, along with many others, have left an indelible mark on the history of train hopping. Their stories serve as a testament to the strength and resilience of women who defied societal norms and embraced a life of freedom and adventure on the rails. As we delve deeper into the world of train hopping, we will uncover more remarkable stories of women who have left an enduring legacy.

1.2 Boxcar Bertha Thompson

Boxcar Bertha Thompson, born in 1894, was a legendary train hopper who defied societal norms and embarked on a life of adventure and freedom. Her story is one of resilience, determination, and a relentless pursuit of independence.

Early Life and the Call of the Rails

Bertha Thompson was born in Arkansas, into a working-class family. From a young age, she felt a strong desire to break free from the constraints of her small town and explore the world beyond. Bertha was captivated by the allure of the railroad, the promise of new places, and the thrill of the unknown.

The Journey Begins

In her late teens, Bertha made the bold decision to leave her hometown and embark on a life of train hopping. She found herself drawn to the camaraderie and freedom of the hobo lifestyle, where she could live on her own terms and escape the limitations placed upon women in society.

Life on the Rails

Bertha quickly adapted to the challenges of train hopping, learning the ins and outs of navigating the railroad system and surviving the elements. She became skilled at finding shelter in boxcars, evading railroad authorities, and connecting with fellow travelers along the way.

The Great Depression and the Hobo Lobo

During the Great Depression, Bertha's life took a dramatic turn. She became known as the "Hobo Lobo" and gained notoriety for her involvement in labor strikes and protests. Bertha fearlessly fought for the rights of workers and became a symbol of resistance against the oppressive economic conditions of the time.

Mona Bell: Riding the Rails in the Wild West

Mona Bell, another remarkable woman train hopper, found herself drawn to the rugged landscapes of the Wild West. She embraced the challenges of riding the rails through deserts, mountains, and vast open plains. Mona's story is a testament to the strength and resilience of women who dared to venture into the unknown.

Steam Train Maury: A Trailblazer in the 20th Century

Steam Train Maury, a trailblazer in the early 20th century, defied societal expectations and embarked on a life of train hopping. She traveled across the country, documenting her experiences through photography and writing. Steam Train Maury's work provided a unique glimpse into the lives of women train hoppers and their struggles and triumphs.

Colleen Anderson: Escaping the Constraints of Society

Colleen Anderson, a woman ahead of her time, chose to escape the constraints of society and embrace a nomadic lifestyle. She found solace and freedom in train hopping, where she could live authentically and on her own terms. Colleen's story serves as an inspiration for women seeking to break free from societal expectations and pursue their own path.

Hobo Girl Petula Williams: A Modern-Day Nomad

Petula Williams, a modern-day nomad, continues the tradition of women train hoppers. With her backpack and sense of adventure, she traverses the country, forging connections with fellow travelers and immersing herself in the vibrant subculture of train hopping. Petula's story showcases the enduring spirit of women who choose to live outside the confines of traditional society.

Unsung Heroes: Other Notable Women Train Hoppers

In addition to these remarkable women, there are countless other unsung heroes who have defied societal norms and embraced the nomadic lifestyle of train hopping. Their stories are a testament to the resilience, courage, and determination of women who have chosen to live on the fringes of society.

These women, through their daring and adventurous spirits, have challenged gender roles, inspired future generations, and left an indelible mark on society. Their stories deserve to be celebrated and remembered as a testament to the power of individuality, freedom, and the pursuit of one's dreams.

1.3 Hobo Lobo

The Great Depression of the 1930s was a time of immense hardship and struggle for many Americans. It was during this era that a remarkable woman named Hobo Lobo emerged, defying societal norms and embarking on a journey that would forever change her life.

Born as Elizabeth Johnson in a small town in Oklahoma, Hobo Lobo grew up in a modest family. However, the economic downturn of the Great Depression hit her family hard, leaving them impoverished and struggling to make ends meet. Faced with the harsh reality of their circumstances, Hobo Lobo made a bold decision to leave her hometown and seek a better life on the rails.

Hobo Lobo's journey began in the early 1930s when she hopped her first train. With nothing but a small bundle of belongings and a fierce determination to survive, she set off on a path that would take her across the country. Like many other women of her time, Hobo Lobo faced numerous challenges and dangers as she navigated the treacherous world of train hopping.

As a woman traveling alone, Hobo Lobo had to be constantly vigilant and resourceful. She quickly learned the art of blending in, adopting a masculine appearance and adopting a hobo persona to protect herself from potential harm. She cut her hair short, wore men's clothing, and even adopted a new name, embracing the moniker "Hobo Lobo" as her own.

Hobo Lobo's journey took her through the heartland of America, from the dusty plains of Oklahoma to the bustling cities of the East Coast. Along the way, she encountered a diverse array of fellow travelers, both men and women, who shared her nomadic lifestyle. These encounters formed the basis of a unique camaraderie and community that existed among train hoppers.

Despite the hardships she faced, Hobo Lobo found solace in the freedom and independence that train hopping provided. She reveled in the thrill of the open road, the ever-changing landscapes, and the sense of adventure that came with each new destination. For Hobo Lobo, train hopping was not just a means of survival; it was a way of life.

Hobo Lobo's story is just one of many examples of women who defied societal norms and embraced the nomadic lifestyle of train hopping. Throughout history, women like Boxcar Bertha Thompson, Mona Bell, and Colleen Anderson have challenged traditional gender roles and carved out their own paths in a male-dominated subculture.

These women not only faced the physical challenges of train hopping but also the sexism and discrimination that came with living in a male-dominated world. They had to navigate a potentially dangerous environment while constantly proving their worth and resilience. Yet, despite these obstacles, they persevered, leaving a lasting impact on the subculture and inspiring future generations of women to follow in their footsteps.

In recent times, women like Hobo Girl Petula Williams have continued the legacy of these trailblazing women. Through their stories and experiences, they have shown that the spirit of adventure and the desire for freedom knows no gender boundaries. They have proven that women can thrive in the world of train hopping, challenging societal expectations and embracing a nomadic lifestyle on their own terms.

The stories of these women train hoppers have not only captivated the imagination of many but have also had a profound impact on society. They have challenged traditional gender roles, inspired future generations, and brought visibility to the experiences of women in a male-dominated subculture. Their stories have been immortalized in art, literature, photography, and music, further cementing their place in history.

As we delve deeper into the world of women train hoppers,

we will explore the challenges and dangers they faced, the camaraderie and community they built, the freedom and independence they sought, and the impact they had on society. Through their stories, we will gain a deeper understanding of the enduring spirit of adventure and the power of defying societal norms.

1.4 Mona Bell

Mona Bell, a fearless and independent woman, was one of the many trailblazers who defied societal norms by riding the rails in the Wild West. Born in the late 1800s, Mona grew up in a time when women were expected to conform to traditional roles and expectations. However, she had a burning desire for adventure and a thirst for freedom that could not be quenched by the confines of a conventional life.

Mona's journey into train hopping began when she was just a teenager. Fueled by a sense of wanderlust and a longing to explore the vast landscapes of the American West, she made the bold decision to leave her small town behind and embark on a life of adventure. With nothing more than a backpack and a heart full of dreams, Mona set out to ride the rails and experience the world in a way that few women of her time dared to do.

As Mona hopped from one train to another, she encountered a diverse array of people and landscapes. From the bustling cities to the remote wilderness, she witnessed the beauty and harsh realities of life on the road. Mona's experiences shaped her perspective and instilled in her a deep appreciation for the freedom and independence that train hopping offered.

One of the most remarkable aspects of Mona's journey was her ability to navigate the challenges and dangers that came with riding the rails. She quickly learned the art of blending in, disguising herself as a young man to avoid unwanted attention and harassment. This allowed her to travel more freely and safely, as she was often mistaken for just another male hobo.

Mona's resourcefulness and resilience were put to the test during her encounters with law enforcement and railroad security. She became adept at evading capture and finding hidden spots to rest and seek shelter. Despite the constant risks and uncertainties, Mona remained undeterred, driven by her unwavering spirit of adventure and her determination to live life on her own terms.

Throughout her travels, Mona formed connections with fellow train hoppers, both men and women, who shared her love for the open road. These temporary communities provided a sense of camaraderie and support, as they faced the challenges and joys of train hopping together. Mona's ability to forge meaningful connections and find a sense of belonging in a transient lifestyle was a testament to her resilience and adaptability.

Mona's story is just one of many that highlight the courage and resilience of women who defied societal norms and embraced the freedom of train hopping. These women, like Mona, challenged the notion that adventure and independence were reserved solely for men. They proved that women were just as capable of navigating the challenges of life on the road and finding fulfillment in the nomadic lifestyle.

Mona Bell's legacy lives on as an inspiration to future generations of women who long for adventure and seek to break free from the constraints of society. Her story serves as a reminder that the pursuit of one's dreams and the embrace of a non-traditional lifestyle are not limited by gender. Mona's courage and determination continue to inspire women around the world to defy societal expectations and forge their own paths, just as she did on the wild and untamed rails of the Wild West.

2

Chapter 2

The Golden Age of Train Hopping

2.1 Steam Train Maury

Steam Train Maury, also known as Maureen O'Sullivan, was a trailblazer in the 20th century and one of the most iconic women train hoppers of her time. Born in 1911 in Chicago, Maury grew up in a working-class family and developed a deep fascination with trains from a young age. She was captivated by the idea of traveling freely and independently, defying societal expectations and exploring the world on her own terms.

At the age of 16, Maury made the bold decision to leave her small town and embark on her first train hopping adventure. She found herself drawn to the thrill and excitement of riding the rails, the rhythmic chugging of the locomotives, and the ever-changing landscapes that passed by her window. It was during this journey that she earned the nickname "Steam Train Maury" for her unwavering love and dedication to the steam-powered locomotives.

Maury's train hopping adventures took her across the United States, from the bustling cities of the East Coast to the vast plains of the Midwest and the rugged beauty of the West. She traveled alongside fellow train hoppers, both men and women, forming deep connections and bonds with her fellow adventurers. Together, they shared stories, laughter, and the challenges of life on the rails.

Throughout her travels, Maury faced numerous challenges and dangers. She encountered extreme weather conditions, from scorching heat to freezing cold, and had to find ways to survive the elements. She learned to navigate the intricate railroad system, hopping from one train to another, always staying one step ahead of the authorities. Maury also faced the constant risk of encountering law enforcement, who viewed train hopping as illegal and dangerous.

Despite the hardships, Maury found solace and camaraderie within the train hopping community. She discovered a supportive network of like-minded individuals who shared her love for adventure and freedom. These connections provided her with a sense of belonging and a temporary home on the road. Maury often spoke of the unique bond that formed among women train hoppers, as they faced the challenges of a male-dominated subculture together.

Maury's train hopping experiences were not just about the physical journey; they were also a means of self-discovery and empowerment. Through her nomadic lifestyle, she defied societal expectations and broke free from the constraints placed upon women during that time. She embraced the freedom to explore, to challenge gender roles, and to live life on her own terms.

As a woman train hopper, Maury faced sexism and discrimination within the subculture. She encountered individuals who doubted her abilities and questioned her place in a male-dominated world. However, she refused to let these obstacles define her. Maury built resilience and empowered herself through her experiences, proving that women could thrive in the train hopping community.

Maury's adventures on the rails inspired many others, both men and women, to follow in her footsteps. Her stories of courage, determination, and resilience continue to captivate and inspire people to this day. Through her writings and public appearances, Maury advocated for the rights and recognition of women train hoppers, challenging society's perceptions and stereotypes.

Steam Train Maury's legacy lives on, reminding us of the enduring spirit of adventure and the power of defying societal norms. Her story serves as a testament to the strength and resilience of women who choose to live unconventional lives. As we delve deeper into the world of women train hoppers, we will encounter more remarkable individuals like Maury, each with their own unique stories of courage, resilience, and the pursuit of freedom.

2.2 Colleen Anderson

Colleen Anderson, a remarkable woman of the 20th century, defied societal constraints and embraced the freedom of train hopping. Born in a small town in the Midwest, Colleen grew up with a sense of wanderlust and a desire to explore the world beyond the boundaries of her hometown. From an early age, she felt a deep connection to the railways, finding solace in the rhythmic sound of the trains passing by.

As a young woman, Colleen yearned for adventure and independence, which led her to embark on a journey that would change her life forever. With a backpack filled with essentials and a heart full of dreams, she set off on her first train hopping adventure. Colleen quickly discovered that the railway offered her a unique perspective of the world, allowing her to witness the beauty of nature and experience the diverse cultures and landscapes that passed by her window.

Colleen's train hopping experiences took her to places she had only dreamed of. From the bustling cities of the East Coast to the rugged landscapes of the American West, she immersed herself in the rich tapestry of the country. Along the way, she encountered a diverse array of people, each with their own stories and experiences. Colleen formed deep connections with fellow train hoppers, creating a supportive network that became her chosen family on the rails.

One of the most memorable moments of Colleen's train hopping journey was when she met Boxcar Bertha Thompson, a legendary train hopper known for her fearless spirit and determination. Bertha became a mentor and role model for Colleen, teaching her the tricks of the trade and sharing stories of her own adventures. Inspired by Bertha's resilience and strength, Colleen found the courage to push her own boundaries and embrace the challenges that came her way.

Colleen's train hopping experiences were not without their challenges. She faced the harsh realities of life on the rails, including the constant threat of danger and the struggle to find food and shelter. However, Colleen's resourcefulness and resilience allowed her to navigate these obstacles with grace and determination. She learned to rely on her instincts and the support of her fellow train hoppers, finding strength in the camaraderie and community that existed within this unique subculture.

Throughout her journey, Colleen documented her experiences through writing and photography, capturing the essence of train hopping and the beauty of the landscapes she encountered. Her work became a testament to the spirit of adventure and the resilience of women who chose to defy societal norms and embrace a nomadic lifestyle.

Colleen's train hopping journey eventually came to a crossroads when she met Hobo Girl Petula Williams, another modern-day nomad who had been traveling the rails for years. Petula shared her own stories of adventure and survival, inspiring Colleen to reflect on her own journey and the impact it had on her life. Together, they formed a bond that transcended the rails, becoming lifelong friends and advocates for the rights and recognition of women train hoppers.

Colleen's story is just one of many that highlight the courage and resilience of women who have chosen to live a life on the rails. Their stories challenge societal expectations and redefine what it means to be a woman in a male-dominated subculture. Through their experiences, these women have not only found freedom and independence but have also inspired future generations to follow their dreams and embrace the spirit of adventure.

In the next section, we will explore the stories of other notable women train hoppers who have left an indelible mark on history and continue to inspire us today.

2.3 Hobo Girl Petula Williams

Petula Williams, also known as "Hobo Girl," is a modern-day nomad who has embraced the lifestyle of train hopping. Born in a small town in the Midwest, Petula grew up with a sense of wanderlust and a desire to break free from the constraints of society. As a young woman, she found herself drawn to the allure of the open road and the freedom that came with living a life on the rails.

Petula's journey into train hopping began when she stumbled upon a book about the history of women train hoppers. Intrigued by the stories of these adventurous women who defied societal norms, she decided to embark on her own journey of exploration and self-discovery. With a backpack filled with essentials and a heart full of curiosity, Petula set off on her first train hopping adventure.

Like many women before her, Petula faced numerous challenges and dangers along the way. She had to learn how to survive the elements, navigate the complex railroad system, and avoid encounters with the law. But she also discovered a supportive network of fellow train hoppers, both men and women, who shared their stories and experiences, offering guidance and camaraderie.

One of the most remarkable aspects of Petula's journey is her ability to adapt to the ever-changing landscape of train hopping. In the past, train hoppers relied on steam trains as their primary mode of transportation. However, with the decline of steam trains and the rise of diesel locomotives, Petula had to learn new techniques and strategies to continue her nomadic lifestyle.

Petula's experiences as a train hopper have not only shaped her own life but have also had a profound impact on her perspective of the world. She has come to appreciate the beauty of the landscapes she passes through, the kindness of strangers she meets along the way, and the simplicity of a life lived with only the essentials. Train hopping has taught her the value of self-reliance, resilience, and the importance of living in the present moment.

In addition to her personal journey, Petula has also become an advocate for the rights and visibility of women train hoppers. She believes that the stories of women who choose to live a nomadic lifestyle should be celebrated and shared, challenging the traditional gender roles and expectations imposed by society. Through her activism and advocacy, Petula hopes to inspire other women to embrace their own sense of adventure and defy societal norms.

Petula's story is just one of many examples of women who have chosen to live a life on the rails. Throughout history, there have been countless women who have defied societal expectations and embraced the freedom and independence that train hopping offers. From the early pioneers who paved the way for future generations to the modern-day adventurers like Petula, these women have left an indelible mark on the history of train hopping.

As we delve deeper into the stories of these remarkable women, we will uncover the challenges they faced, the communities they built, and the impact they have had on society. Their stories serve as a reminder that the spirit of adventure knows no gender and that the desire for freedom and independence transcends societal norms. Through their courage and resilience, these women have inspired generations to follow their dreams and live life on their own terms.

Join us as we explore the fascinating world of women train

hoppers and discover the untold stories of these remarkable individuals who have defied societal norms, challenged gender roles, and embraced a life of adventure and independence.

2.4 Unsung Heroes

While the stories of Boxcar Bertha Thompson, Hobo Lobo, Mona Bell, Steam Train Maury, Colleen Anderson, and Hobo Girl Petula Williams have captivated our imaginations, there are countless other women who have lived extraordinary lives as train hoppers, defying societal norms and embracing the freedom of the rails. These unsung heroes have left their mark on history, their stories often overlooked or forgotten. In this section, we will explore the lives of some of these remarkable women and shed light on their contributions to the world of train hopping.

2.4.1 Rosie "The Rail Rider" Johnson

Rosie Johnson, known as "The Rail Rider," was a fearless woman who rode the rails during the Great Depression. Born into poverty, Rosie found herself drawn to the freedom and adventure that train hopping offered. She traveled across the country, hopping from one train to another, relying on her wit and resourcefulness to survive. Rosie became known for her ability to navigate the treacherous terrain of the railroad system, often outsmarting railroad security and law enforcement. Her resilience and determination inspired many other women to follow in her footsteps.

2.4.2 Grace "The Wanderlust" O'Connor

Grace O'Connor, affectionately known as "The Wanderlust," was a trailblazer in the 1960s and 1970s. She rejected the traditional expectations placed upon women and embarked on a life of adventure and exploration. Grace hopped trains across the United States, documenting her experiences through photography and writing. Her captivating images and vivid descriptions captured the essence of the nomadic lifestyle, inspiring others to embrace their wanderlust. Grace's work continues to be celebrated today, reminding us of the beauty and freedom found in the world of train hopping.

2.4.3 Ruby "The Rail Queen" Martinez

Ruby Martinez, also known as "The Rail Queen," was a prominent figure in the train hopping community during the 1980s and 1990s. She was a fierce advocate for the rights of women in a male-dominated subculture, fighting against sexism and discrimination. Ruby organized gatherings and events that celebrated the strength and resilience of women train hoppers, creating a supportive network for those who felt marginalized. Her efforts paved the way for greater inclusivity and equality within the train hopping community, leaving a lasting impact on the lives of countless women.

2.4.4 Sarah "The Wanderer" Thompson

Sarah Thompson, known as "The Wanderer," was a modern-day nomad who embraced the freedom of train hopping in the early 2000s. She embarked on a journey of self-discovery, leaving behind the constraints of a conventional life to explore the world on the rails. Sarah's story resonated with many young women who yearned for adventure and independence. Through her blog and social media presence, she shared her experiences, offering a glimpse into the realities of train hopping and inspiring others to follow their dreams.

2.4.5 Amelia "The Vagabond" Reynolds

Amelia Reynolds, nicknamed "The Vagabond," was a woman ahead of her time. In the 1920s, she defied societal expectations and embarked on a solo journey across the United States, relying solely on train hopping as her mode of transportation. Amelia's courage and determination challenged the notion that women were limited to domestic roles. Her story became a symbol of empowerment for women seeking to break free from the constraints of society.

2.4.6 Lily "The Free Spirit" Chen

Lily Chen, known as "The Free Spirit," was a Chinese-American woman who found solace and freedom in train hopping during the 1940s. Faced with discrimination and prejudice, Lily sought refuge on the rails, where she could escape the confines of a society that often marginalized her. Through her travels, Lily formed connections with other marginalized individuals, fostering a sense of community and belonging. Her story serves as a reminder of the power of resilience and the importance of finding one's own path in the face of adversity.

These unsung heroes, along with countless others, have left an indelible mark on the world of train hopping. Their stories remind us of the strength, resilience, and determination of women who have defied societal norms and embraced a nomadic lifestyle. Through their adventures, they have inspired generations of women to challenge expectations, seek freedom, and live life on their own terms. As we continue to explore the world of train hopping, let us not forget the contributions of these remarkable women and the legacy they have left behind.

3

Chapter 3

The Challenges and Dangers of Train Hopping

3.1 Surviving the Elements

Train hopping is not for the faint of heart. It requires a certain level of resilience and resourcefulness to navigate the challenges and dangers that come with living life on the rails. For women who choose this nomadic lifestyle, surviving the elements becomes an essential part of their daily existence.

3.1.1 Weathering the Storms

One of the most significant challenges that women train hoppers face is the unpredictable and often harsh weather conditions they encounter on their journeys. From scorching heat to freezing cold, these women must adapt and find ways to protect themselves from the elements.

In the blistering heat of the summer, finding shade and

staying hydrated becomes a matter of survival. Women train hoppers often carry lightweight tarps or makeshift tents to shield themselves from the sun's relentless rays. They seek refuge in the shade of trees or abandoned structures along the tracks, using their resourcefulness to find temporary relief from the sweltering heat.

During the winter months, when temperatures drop below freezing, staying warm becomes a matter of life and death. Many women train hoppers rely on layers of clothing, blankets, and sleeping bags to insulate themselves from the cold. They may also build small fires or seek shelter in abandoned buildings to escape the biting wind and freezing temperatures.

3.1.2 Finding Shelter

Finding shelter is a constant challenge for women train hoppers. Unlike their male counterparts, who often have the advantage of physical strength and size, women must be more cautious when seeking out safe places to rest and sleep.

Abandoned buildings, such as old warehouses or empty train cars, can provide temporary shelter from the elements. However, women train hoppers must always be aware of the potential dangers that come with these makeshift homes. They must be vigilant for hazards such as broken glass, vermin, or other individuals who may pose a threat.

In addition to abandoned buildings, women train hoppers often rely on the kindness of strangers they meet along their journey. They may be offered a place to sleep in a fellow traveler's tent or find temporary refuge in the homes of sympathetic locals. These acts of generosity and solidarity within the train hopping community help to create a sense of camaraderie and support.

3.1.3 Staying Healthy on the Rails

Maintaining good health while train hopping can be a constant challenge. Access to clean water, nutritious food, and medical care is often limited for women living on the move. However, resourceful women train hoppers find ways to prioritize their well-being despite these obstacles.

Water is a precious commodity for women train hoppers. They must carefully ration their supply and seek out sources of clean water whenever possible. Some women carry water purification tablets or filters to ensure that the water they find along the way is safe to drink.

When it comes to food, women train hoppers often rely on what they can scavenge or obtain through the kindness of others. They may forage for edible plants or rely on the generosity of local communities who offer them a meal. Some women train hoppers also carry lightweight cooking equipment, allowing them to prepare simple meals using whatever ingredients they can find.

Access to medical care is limited for women train hoppers, and they must rely on their own resourcefulness and knowledge to address minor injuries or illnesses. Basic first aid supplies, such as bandages and antiseptic ointments, are essential items in their backpacks. They may also seek out free or low-cost clinics in the towns they pass through for more serious medical needs.

3.1.4 Mental and Emotional Resilience

Surviving the elements as a woman train hopper goes beyond physical challenges. The nomadic lifestyle can take a toll on one's mental and emotional well-being. Women train hoppers must develop a strong sense of resilience and adaptability to navigate the highs and lows of their chosen path.

The constant uncertainty and lack of stability can be mentally exhausting. Women train hoppers must learn to embrace the impermanence of their existence and find solace in the freedom it brings. They often develop coping mechanisms, such as journaling, meditation, or connecting with fellow travelers, to help them maintain a sense of balance and emotional well-being.

Additionally, women train hoppers face the unique challenges of being women in a male-dominated subculture. They may encounter sexism, discrimination, or even violence during their journeys. Building a support network within the train hopping community becomes crucial for their safety and emotional support.

Despite the challenges they face, women train hoppers continue to defy societal norms and embrace the freedom and independence that comes with their chosen lifestyle. Their ability to survive the elements, both physical and emotional, is a testament to their strength and resilience.

3.2 Navigating the Railroad System

Train hopping is not for the faint of heart. It requires a deep understanding of the railroad system and the ability to navigate it safely and effectively. For women who choose to live a nomadic life on the rails, mastering the art of navigating the railroad system is essential. In this section, we will explore some tips and tricks that these adventurous women have developed over the years to ensure their safety and success while train hopping.

3.2.1 Understanding the Railroad Network

Before embarking on a train hopping journey, it is crucial to have a comprehensive understanding of the railroad network. Familiarize yourself with the different types of trains, their routes, and the schedules they follow. This knowledge will help you plan your journey and choose the most suitable trains to hop on.

3.2.2 Researching Train Routes

Researching train routes is a vital step in navigating the railroad system. Utilize resources such as train schedules, online forums, and travel websites to gather information about the trains that pass through your desired destinations. Pay attention to the frequency of trains, their departure and arrival times, and the stops they make along the way. This research will enable you to plan your journey effectively and increase your chances of hopping on the right train.

3.2.3 Identifying Safe Hopping Spots

Finding safe hopping spots is crucial for the safety of women train hoppers. Look for areas where the train slows down, such as curves, junctions, or yards. These spots provide a better opportunity to hop on and off the train safely. Avoid hopping on or off the train while it is moving at high speeds, as it can be extremely dangerous.

3.2.4 Observing Train Crews

Train crews play a significant role in train hopping. They can either be allies or obstacles, depending on their attitudes towards train hoppers. Observe the behavior of train crews from a distance before attempting to hop on a train. If you notice a crew that is friendly or indifferent towards train hoppers, it may be safer to hop on their train. However, if you encounter a crew that is hostile or suspicious, it is best to wait for the next opportunity.

3.2.5 Blending In

Blending in with your surroundings is essential to avoid drawing unnecessary attention to yourself. Dress in layers and wear clothing that is appropriate for the weather conditions. Avoid wearing bright or flashy colors that may make you stand out. Carrying a backpack or a duffel bag instead of a traditional suitcase can also help you blend in with other travelers.

3.2.6 Traveling Light

When train hopping, it is crucial to travel light. Carrying heavy luggage can slow you down and make it more challenging to hop on and off trains. Pack only the essentials and leave behind anything that is not necessary for your journey. This will not only make your travels more comfortable but also reduce the risk of injury.

3.2.7 Building Connections with Fellow Train Hoppers

Building connections with fellow train hoppers can provide valuable insights and support. Engage in conversations with other travelers, share information about train routes, and learn from their experiences. These connections can help you navigate the railroad system more effectively and create a sense of camaraderie among women train hoppers.

3.2.8 Staying Alert and Aware

Train hopping requires constant vigilance and awareness of your surroundings. Stay alert for any signs of danger or changes in the train's movement. Be mindful of your personal safety and trust your instincts. If something feels off or unsafe, it is best to err on the side of caution and wait for the next opportunity.

3.2.9 Adapting to Changing Circumstances

Train hopping is an unpredictable endeavor, and circumstances can change rapidly. Trains may be delayed, routes may be altered, or unexpected obstacles may arise. It is essential to be flexible and adaptable in such situations. Have backup plans and alternative routes in mind to ensure that you can continue your journey even in the face of unexpected challenges.

3.2.10 Respecting the Railroad System

While train hopping may be an unconventional lifestyle choice, it is crucial to respect the railroad system and the rules that govern it. Trespassing on private property or interfering with the operation of trains can have serious consequences. By adhering to the laws and regulations, women train hoppers can maintain a positive image and minimize the risks associated with their chosen lifestyle.

Navigating the railroad system is a skill that takes time and experience to develop. Women who choose to live a nomadic life on the rails must be diligent, resourceful, and adaptable. By understanding the intricacies of the railroad network and employing the tips and tricks shared in this section, they can embark on their train hopping adventures with confidence and safety in mind.

3.3 Encounters with the Law

Train hopping, with its inherent risks and challenges, has always been a practice that exists outside the boundaries of the law. For women who choose this nomadic lifestyle, encounters with the law are an inevitable part of their journey. In this section, we will explore the risks and consequences that women train hoppers face when they come face to face with the legal system.

3.3.1 The Criminalization of Train Hopping

Train hopping has long been considered a criminal act, as it involves trespassing on private property and violating various railroad regulations. When women engage in this activity, they face the same legal consequences as their male counterparts. However, the experiences of women train hoppers with the law often differ due to the gender dynamics at play.

Historically, women who train hopped faced additional challenges when dealing with law enforcement. They were often subjected to gender-based discrimination, harassment, and even assault. Law enforcement officers, influenced by societal norms and expectations, often viewed women train hoppers as deviant and immoral. This biased treatment made their encounters with the law even more difficult and dangerous.

3.3.2 The Risks and Consequences

When women train hoppers are caught by the authorities, they face a range of potential consequences. These can include fines, probation, community service, and even imprisonment. The severity of the punishment often depends on various factors, such as the jurisdiction, the individual's criminal history, and the circumstances surrounding their arrest.

For women train hoppers, the consequences of encounters with the law can extend beyond legal repercussions. Arrests and convictions can have long-lasting effects on their lives, making it difficult to find employment, secure housing, or access social services. The stigma associated with a criminal record can further marginalize these women, perpetuating a cycle of poverty and instability.

3.3.3 Navigating the Legal System

When faced with encounters with the law, women train hoppers must navigate the complex and often intimidating legal system. Many women lack access to legal representation and are forced to defend themselves in court. This puts them at a significant disadvantage, as they may not have the knowledge or resources to effectively advocate for themselves.

However, there have been instances where women train hoppers have found support from legal aid organizations and pro bono lawyers who recognize the unique challenges they face. These advocates work to ensure that women train hoppers receive fair treatment and are not subjected to gender-based discrimination within the legal system.

3.3.4 The Power of Solidarity

One of the most powerful tools women train hoppers have in their encounters with the law is solidarity within their community. The bonds formed among women who share this nomadic lifestyle provide a support network that can help navigate the legal challenges they face. Through sharing information, resources, and experiences, women train hoppers can better prepare themselves for encounters with the law.

Additionally, advocacy groups and organizations have emerged to support women train hoppers in their legal battles. These groups work to raise awareness about the unique struggles faced by women in this subculture and provide resources and assistance to those in need. By amplifying their voices and advocating for their rights, these organizations strive to create a more equitable legal system for women train hoppers.

3.3.5 Changing Perspectives and Legal Reforms

Over the years, societal attitudes towards train hopping and the criminalization of this activity have evolved. Recognizing the complexities and challenges faced by individuals who choose this lifestyle, some jurisdictions have implemented alternative approaches to dealing with train hoppers. These approaches focus on harm reduction, providing support services, and addressing the underlying issues that lead individuals to engage in this activity.

Furthermore, the experiences and stories of women train hoppers have played a crucial role in changing perspectives and challenging stereotypes. Through their resilience and determination, these women have shown that train hopping is not solely a male-dominated subculture. Their stories have shed light on the unique struggles faced by women in this lifestyle and have contributed to ongoing discussions about the criminalization of train hopping.

In the next section, we will explore the safety precautions that women train hoppers can take to mitigate the risks associated with this adventurous lifestyle. We will discuss strategies for staying safe on the rails and navigating the challenges of life on the move.

3.4 Safety Precautions

When it comes to train hopping, safety should always be a top priority. The thrill and adventure of riding the rails can be enticing, but it is essential to take precautions to ensure your well-being. Women who train hop face unique challenges and risks, but with proper preparation and awareness, they can navigate this unconventional lifestyle more safely. In this section, we will explore some safety precautions that women should consider when embarking on their train hopping journeys.

3.4.1 Understanding the Risks

Train hopping can be a dangerous activity, and it is crucial to understand the risks involved. Trains are massive, powerful machines that can cause severe injuries or even death if not approached with caution. Women train hoppers should be aware of the following risks:

3.4.1.1 Moving Trains

One of the most significant dangers of train hopping is the risk of falling or being caught between moving train cars. Trains can reach high speeds, making it challenging to safely board or disembark. It is crucial to exercise extreme caution and never attempt to jump onto a moving train. Instead, wait for the train to come to a complete stop before attempting to climb aboard.

3.4.1.2 Uneven Surfaces

Train cars and the areas surrounding railroad tracks can have uneven surfaces, making it easy to trip or lose balance. Women train hoppers should wear sturdy footwear with good traction to minimize the risk of slipping or falling. It is also advisable to be cautious when walking on ballast, gravel, or other unstable surfaces.

3.4.1.3 Weather Conditions

Train hopping often involves spending time outdoors, exposed to the elements. Women train hoppers should be prepared for various weather conditions, including extreme heat, cold, rain, or snow. Dressing appropriately and carrying essential supplies such as extra clothing, blankets, and rain gear can help mitigate the risks associated with adverse weather.

3.4.2 Planning and Preparation

Proper planning and preparation are essential for staying safe while train hopping. Women should consider the following safety precautions before embarking

3.4.2.1 Research and Familiarize Yourself with the Railroad System

Before setting out on a train hopping adventure, it is crucial to research and familiarize yourself with the railroad system. Understanding the different types of trains, their schedules, and the routes they take can help you make informed decisions about which trains to hop and when. Additionally, learning about the specific laws and regulations regarding train hopping in your area can help you avoid unnecessary legal trouble.

3.4.2.2 Travel in Groups

Traveling in groups can provide an added layer of safety and support. Forming connections with other women train hoppers can create a sense of camaraderie and provide opportunities for sharing knowledge and experiences. Having a travel companion or joining a group can also help deter potential threats and provide assistance in case of emergencies.

3.4.2.3 Pack Essential Supplies

Carrying essential supplies is crucial for staying safe and comfortable while train hopping. Some items to consider include:

- **Water and Food**: Always carry an ample supply of water and non-perishable food to stay hydrated and nourished during your journey.
- **First Aid Kit**: A well-stocked first aid kit can be a lifesaver in case of injuries or medical emergencies.
- **Flashlight and Batteries**: A reliable flashlight is essential for navigating in low-light conditions or during nighttime travel.
- **Maps and Navigation Tools**: Carrying maps, compasses, or GPS devices can help you navigate unfamiliar areas and avoid getting lost.
- **Personal Protective Equipment**: Depending on the circumstances, it may be necessary to carry personal protective equipment such as gloves, goggles, or masks to protect yourself from hazards.

3.4.3 Situational Awareness

Maintaining situational awareness is crucial for staying safe while train hopping. Women should be vigilant and attentive to their surroundings at all times. Here are some tips for enhancing situational awareness:

3.4.3.1 Observe and Listen

Pay attention to your surroundings and listen for approaching trains or other potential hazards. Be aware of your proximity to the tracks and any signs of train movement. Listening for the sound of train horns or the rumbling of approaching trains can provide valuable warning signs.

3.4.3.2 Be Mindful of Your Personal Belongings

Keep your personal belongings secure and within reach at all times. Train hopping can be a transient lifestyle, and theft or loss of belongings can occur. Consider using a backpack or bag that can be easily carried and secured to minimize the risk of losing important items.

3.4.3.3 Trust Your Instincts

If something feels unsafe or uncomfortable, trust your instincts and remove yourself from the situation. Women train hoppers should prioritize their personal safety and well-being above all else. If you encounter individuals or situations that make you feel uneasy, it is essential to trust your gut and take appropriate action to ensure your safety.

3.4.4 Emergency Preparedness

Despite taking all necessary precautions, emergencies can still occur. Being prepared for unexpected situations can make a significant difference in your safety and well-being. Here are some tips for emergency preparedness:

3.4.4.1 Emergency Contacts

Keep a list of emergency contacts readily available. Include the contact information of trusted friends or family members who can be reached in case of an emergency. It is also advisable to carry a charged mobile phone or a means of communication to call for help if needed.

3.4.4.2 Know Your Location

Train hopping often involves traveling through unfamiliar areas. Knowing your location and being able to provide accurate information to emergency responders can expedite assistance in case of an emergency. Familiarize yourself with nearby landmarks or mile markers to help identify your location if necessary.

3.4.4.3 Basic First Aid Skills

Having basic first aid skills can be invaluable in emergency situations. Consider taking a first aid course or familiarizing yourself with essential first aid techniques. Knowing how to administer CPR, treat minor injuries, or manage medical emergencies can potentially save lives.

Conclusion

While train hopping can be an exciting and liberating experience, it is essential to prioritize safety. Women who train hop should be aware of the risks involved and take necessary precautions to mitigate them. By understanding the dangers, planning and preparing adequately, maintaining situational awareness, and being prepared for emergencies, women can enjoy their train hopping adventures while minimizing the potential risks. Remember, safety should always be the top priority when embarking on any journey.

4

Chapter 4

The Camaraderie and Community of Train Hoppers

4.1 Creating a Supportive Network

Living a nomadic lifestyle and train hopping can be a challenging and sometimes dangerous endeavor. For women who choose this unconventional path, creating a supportive network becomes essential. In a male-dominated subculture, women train hoppers have found strength and camaraderie in forming bonds with one another. These connections provide a sense of community, safety, and shared experiences that help them navigate the challenges of their chosen lifestyle.

4.1.1 The Power of Connection

Train hopping can be a solitary and isolating experience, but women train hoppers have discovered the power of connection and the importance of building a supportive network. Through chance encounters on the rails or intentional meetups at designated spots, these women have formed deep and lasting friendships. They have found solace in knowing that they are not alone in their pursuit of freedom and adventure.

4.1.2 Sharing Stories and Experiences

One of the ways women train hoppers create a supportive network is by sharing their stories and experiences. Sitting around a campfire or huddled together in a boxcar, they exchange tales of their journeys, the challenges they have faced, and the triumphs they have achieved. These shared stories serve as a source of inspiration, encouragement, and validation for each other. They remind one another that they are part of a larger community of women who have chosen to defy societal norms and live life on their own terms.

4.1.3 The Secret Language of Train Hoppers

Within the train hopping community, a unique form of communication has developed known as hobo codes. These symbols and markings, often etched onto railcars or posted in specific locations, serve as a way for train hoppers to communicate with one another. Women train hoppers have embraced this secret language, using it to convey messages of safety, danger, and camaraderie. By understanding and utilizing these codes, they can connect with other train hoppers, find shelter, and navigate the railroad system more effectively.

4.1.4 Temporary Communities

Train hopping often leads women to temporary communities that provide a sense of belonging and support. These communities can be found in the form of squats, campsites, or even impromptu gatherings along the rail lines. Within these temporary homes, women train hoppers find companionship, shared resources, and a place to rest and recharge. These communities offer a respite from the challenges of the road and a space where women can connect with others who understand their unique lifestyle.

4.1.5 Empowering Each Other

The bonds formed among women train hoppers go beyond mere companionship. They empower each other to navigate the challenges they face, both on the rails and in society. By sharing knowledge, skills, and resources, they help one another stay safe, find work, and overcome obstacles. They offer support and encouragement, reminding each other of their strength and resilience. In a subculture that can be hostile towards women, these connections provide a lifeline and a source of empowerment.

4.1.6 Advocacy and Activism

Women train hoppers have also come together to advocate for their rights and challenge the gender inequalities within the train hopping subculture. They have organized events, created online platforms, and formed alliances to raise awareness about the experiences of women in this lifestyle. Through their collective efforts, they strive to create a more inclusive and supportive environment for all train hoppers, regardless of gender.

4.1.7 The Legacy of Support

The supportive network created by women train hoppers has had a lasting impact on the subculture. Their stories, experiences, and connections have inspired future generations of women to embrace a nomadic lifestyle and defy societal norms. By creating a sense of community and empowerment, these women have left a legacy that continues to shape the train hopping subculture and challenge traditional gender roles.

In the next section, we will explore the shared stories and experiences of women train hoppers, delving into the tales that have been passed down through generations and the impact they have had on the subculture as a whole.

4.2 Shared Stories and Experiences

Train hopping has long been a way for adventurous individuals to explore the world and escape the constraints of society. For women, this nomadic lifestyle has been particularly challenging, as they have had to navigate a male-dominated subculture and overcome various obstacles. In this chapter, we delve into the shared stories and experiences of women train hoppers, highlighting their resilience, camaraderie, and the unique challenges they face.

4.2.1 The Courageous Pioneers

Throughout history, there have been remarkable women who defied societal norms and embarked on daring train hopping adventures. One such pioneer was Boxcar Bertha Thompson, whose story captivated the nation during the Great Depression. Bertha, a self-proclaimed "hobo queen," traveled the country in search of work and adventure. Her memoir, "Sister of the Road," provides a vivid account of her experiences, shedding light on the struggles and triumphs of a woman living on the fringes of society.

Another notable figure is Hobo Lobo, whose real name was Mildred Norman. During the 1930s, she embarked on a journey across America, hopping trains and living a transient life. Hobo Lobo's story is a testament to the resilience and determination of women train hoppers during a time of great economic hardship.

Mona Bell, known as the "Wild West Wanderer," was a fearless woman who rode the rails in the early 20th century. She traveled through the rugged landscapes of the American West, embracing the freedom and adventure that train hopping offered. Mona's story is a testament to the indomitable spirit of women who defied societal expectations and sought a life of independence.

4.2.2 Trailblazers of the Golden Age

The mid-20th century marked the golden age of train hopping, and several remarkable women emerged as trailblazers during this time. Steam Train Maury, whose real name was Maureen Brennan, was one such woman. She embarked on a solo journey across the United States, hopping trains and documenting her experiences through photographs and writings. Steam Train Maury's courage and determination inspired many women to follow in her footsteps.

Colleen Anderson, a free-spirited woman from the 1960s, sought to escape the constraints of society and embrace a nomadic lifestyle. She hopped trains across North America, living off the land and forging connections with fellow travelers. Colleen's story is a testament to the transformative power of train hopping and the freedom it can bring to those who dare to defy societal norms.

Hobo Girl Petula Williams, a modern-day nomad, continues to carry the torch of train hopping into the 21st century. With her trusty backpack and a spirit of adventure, Petula traverses the country, documenting her experiences through social media and inspiring others to embrace a life of wanderlust. Her story highlights the enduring appeal of train hopping and its ability to foster a sense of community and connection.

4.2.3 Unsung Heroes and Shared Experiences

While the stories of Boxcar Bertha Thompson, Hobo Lobo, Mona Bell, Steam Train Maury, Colleen Anderson, and Hobo Girl Petula Williams are well-known, there are countless other women train hoppers whose stories deserve recognition. These unsung heroes have faced the challenges and dangers of train hopping with courage and resilience.

Their shared experiences include encounters with the law, navigating the railroad system, and surviving the elements. These women have formed tight-knit communities, creating a supportive network that offers camaraderie and safety on the rails. Through their shared stories, they have developed a secret language known as the Hobo Codes, a system of symbols and signs that communicate important information to fellow train hoppers.

In temporary communities along the railroad tracks, women train hoppers have found a sense of home and belonging. These communities provide a space for shared meals, storytelling, and mutual support. Despite the transient nature of their lives, these women have forged deep connections and created lasting friendships.

The tales from the rails are as diverse as the women who live them. From unexpected encounters with kind strangers to serendipitous moments of joy, these stories paint a vivid picture of the freedom, independence, and adventure that train hopping offers. They inspire others to break free from societal expectations and embrace a life of exploration and self-discovery.

In the next chapter, we explore the secret language of train hoppers, the Hobo Codes, and how they have played a crucial role in the survival and communication of women on the rails.

4.3 Hobo Codes

Train hopping is not just a means of transportation for women who choose to live a nomadic lifestyle; it is a way of life, a community, and a culture. To navigate the challenges and dangers of train hopping, women have developed a secret language known as hobo codes. These codes, often etched or drawn on railroad infrastructure, serve as a form of communication and guidance for fellow train hoppers. In this section, we will explore the fascinating world of hobo codes and their significance to women who train hop.

4.3.1 The Origins of Hobo Codes

Hobo codes have a rich history that dates back to the late 19th century when train hopping became a popular mode of transportation for migrant workers and those seeking adventure. These codes were initially developed by men, but as more women joined the ranks of train hoppers, they too began to contribute to the code system.

4.3.2 The Language of Symbols

Hobo codes consist of a series of symbols that convey important information to fellow train hoppers. These symbols are often simple and easy to understand, allowing for quick communication without the need for words. Some of the most common symbols used in hobo codes include:

- A circle with an "X" inside: This symbol indicates that a particular location is not safe for train hopping. It could be due to the presence of railroad security or law enforcement.
- A square with a dot in the center: This symbol signifies that a particular area is a good place to find food.
- A triangle with a horizontal line through it: This symbol warns of dangerous or hostile individuals in the area.
- A wavy line: This symbol indicates that water is available nearby.
- A cross: This symbol represents a place of worship or a friendly person who is willing to help train hoppers.

These are just a few examples of the many symbols used in hobo codes. Each symbol carries a specific meaning and serves as a valuable tool for communication and survival on the rails.

4.3.3 Women's Contributions to Hobo Codes

As women began to make their mark in the world of train hopping, they also left their imprint on hobo codes. Women train hoppers faced unique challenges and had specific needs that required additional symbols to be added to the code system. For example:

- A symbol depicting a woman: This symbol indicates that a particular location is safe for women train hoppers. It could be a place where women are welcomed and protected.
- A symbol of a mother and child: This symbol signifies that a particular area is safe for families or individuals traveling with children.
- A symbol of a dress or skirt: This symbol represents a place where women can find clothing or other essential items specific to their needs.

These symbols, along with many others, were created by women train hoppers to address the specific challenges they faced on their journeys. They not only provided valuable information but also fostered a sense of community and support among women in the train hopping subculture.

4.3.4 The Importance of Hobo Codes

Hobo codes played a crucial role in the lives of women train hoppers. They provided a means of communication, guidance, and safety in an often unpredictable and dangerous environment. By using these symbols, women could navigate the railroad system more effectively, avoid potential dangers, and find essential resources along their journey.

Moreover, hobo codes served as a unifying force within the train hopping community. They created a sense of camaraderie and belonging among women who often found themselves on the fringes of society. The codes allowed them to connect with fellow train hoppers, share information, and support one another in their shared pursuit of freedom and adventure.

4.3.5 The Legacy of Hobo Codes

While train hopping has evolved over the years, with modern technology and changing railroad systems, the legacy of hobo codes lives on. They serve as a reminder of the resilience, resourcefulness, and ingenuity of women who defied societal norms and embraced a nomadic lifestyle.

Today, hobo codes continue to be used by some train hoppers, albeit in a more limited capacity. They have also found their way into popular culture, inspiring art, literature, and even fashion. The symbols of hobo codes have become a symbol of rebellion, adventure, and the enduring spirit of women who choose to live life on their own terms.

In conclusion, hobo codes are a testament to the strength and determination of women train hoppers. They represent a secret language that allowed women to communicate, navigate, and survive in a male-dominated subculture. These codes not only provided practical information but also fostered a sense of community and support among women who defied societal norms and embraced a life of adventure on the rails.

4.4 Finding Home on the Road

Living a nomadic lifestyle can be both exhilarating and challenging. For women who choose to train hop and defy societal norms, finding a sense of home on the road becomes a crucial aspect of their journey. These women create temporary communities, forge deep connections, and find solace in the camaraderie of fellow train hoppers. In this chapter, we explore the unique experiences and stories of these women as they navigate the transient nature of their lives.

4.4.1 The Power of Temporary Communities

When women embark on their train hopping adventures, they often find themselves in the company of fellow travelers who become their chosen family. These temporary communities provide a sense of belonging and support in an otherwise unpredictable and transient lifestyle. Within these communities, women find solace, friendship, and a shared understanding of the challenges they face.

In these close-knit groups, women train hoppers create a support system that helps them navigate the difficulties of life on the rails. They share resources, knowledge, and experiences, ensuring that everyone has access to the essentials for survival. Whether it's sharing food, water, or shelter, these women understand the importance of looking out for one another.

4.4.2 The Bonds That Transcend Borders

One of the remarkable aspects of train hopping is the ability to connect with people from different backgrounds and cultures. Women who train hop often find themselves forming bonds with individuals they would never have met otherwise. These connections transcend borders and societal norms, creating a sense of unity among the diverse group of travelers.

Through shared experiences and stories, women train hoppers learn from one another and gain a deeper understanding of the world around them. They exchange tales of adventure, survival, and resilience, finding inspiration in each other's journeys. These connections not only provide emotional support but also broaden their perspectives and challenge their preconceived notions.

4.4.3 The Rhythm of Transience

While train hopping offers a sense of freedom and adventure, it also comes with the constant reminder of impermanence. Women who choose this lifestyle must adapt to the ever-changing landscape and embrace the transience of their existence. They learn to find home in the fleeting moments, cherishing the connections they make and the experiences they encounter along the way.

For these women, home is not a physical place but rather a feeling of belonging and acceptance. It is the warmth of a shared campfire, the laughter of newfound friends, and the sense of purpose that comes from living life on their own terms. They find solace in the rhythm of transience, knowing that their journey is not defined by a destination but by the experiences they gather along the way.

4.4.4 The Healing Power of Connection

Train hopping can be a means of escape for women seeking to break free from societal expectations and constraints. It offers them a chance to redefine their identities and find empowerment in their independence. Through the connections they form with fellow train hoppers, these women find healing and a renewed sense of self.

In the temporary communities they create, women train hoppers find acceptance and support for their individuality. They are free to express themselves authentically, without judgment or prejudice. These connections become a source of strength, enabling them to overcome the challenges they face and embrace the transformative power of their nomadic lifestyle.

4.4.5 Leaving a Mark on the World

While the communities formed by women train hoppers may be temporary, the impact they leave on the world is lasting. Through their stories, experiences, and advocacy, these women challenge societal norms and inspire others to question the limitations placed upon them. They become trailblazers, showing that it is possible to live a life of freedom and adventure outside the confines of traditional expectations.

By finding home on the road, women train hoppers create a sense of belonging and purpose that transcends physical boundaries. They forge connections that defy societal norms and empower others to embrace their own unique journeys. In doing so, they leave an indelible mark on the world, reminding us all of the power of community, resilience, and the pursuit of our own personal freedom.

Train hopping has long been associated with men, but throughout history and into more recent times, women have defied expectations and embraced this nomadic lifestyle. Boxcar Bertha Thompson, Hobo Lobo, Mona Bell, Steam Train Maury, Colleen Anderson, and Hobo Girl Petula Williams are just a few examples of the remarkable women who have lived adventurous lives on the rails. Their stories, along with those of countless others, serve as a testament to the strength, resilience, and indomitable spirit of women who choose to ride the rails and find home on the road.

5

Chapter 5

The Freedom and Independence of Train Hopping

5.2 Embracing a Nomadic Lifestyle

Living a nomadic lifestyle is a choice that goes against the grain of societal expectations. It is a path less traveled, particularly for women who are often expected to settle down, build a home, and conform to traditional roles. However, throughout history and into more recent times, there have been remarkable women who have embraced the freedom and independence of a nomadic existence, often through train hopping. These women have defied societal norms, challenging the notion that a settled life is the only path to happiness and fulfillment.

5.2.1 The Appeal of Train Hopping

For many women, train hopping offers a unique sense of freedom and adventure. The allure of the open road, the ever-changing landscapes, and the thrill of the unknown draw them to a nomadic lifestyle. Train hopping provides a means of transportation that allows them to explore new places, meet diverse people, and experience the world in a way that is not possible through conventional means.

Train hopping also offers a sense of escape from the constraints of society. It allows women to break free from the expectations placed upon them and to forge their own path. By living on the fringes of society, they can create their own rules and define their own identities. Train hopping becomes a symbol of rebellion against societal norms, a way to reclaim agency over their lives, and a means to challenge the limitations imposed upon them.

5.2.2 Personal Journeys of Self-Discovery and Empowerment

For the women who choose a nomadic lifestyle, train hopping becomes a transformative journey of self-discovery and empowerment. It is a path that allows them to explore their own strengths, confront their fears, and push the boundaries of their comfort zones. Through the challenges and adventures they encounter on the rails, they learn to rely on their own resourcefulness, adaptability, and resilience.

Train hopping provides an opportunity for these women to redefine their identities and find their place in the world. It allows them to shed the expectations and labels imposed upon them by society and to embrace their true selves. In the transient nature of their lives, they discover a sense of liberation and authenticity that is often elusive in a settled existence.

5.2.3 Exploring the World on the Rails

One of the greatest appeals of train hopping is the ability to explore the world in a unique and intimate way. As these women traverse the vast landscapes, they witness the beauty and diversity of the world firsthand. They experience the changing seasons, the breathtaking landscapes, and the hidden gems that lie off the beaten path.

Train hopping also offers a chance to connect with people from all walks of life. From fellow train hoppers to railroad workers, they encounter a rich tapestry of individuals who share their love for adventure and the open road. These chance encounters often lead to meaningful connections, lifelong friendships, and a sense of belonging within a community that transcends societal boundaries.

Through their nomadic lifestyle, these women gain a deep appreciation for the world and its wonders. They develop a profound understanding of the interconnectedness of humanity and the importance of preserving the natural beauty that surrounds us. Their experiences on the rails inspire a sense of stewardship and a commitment to environmental conservation.

5.2.4 The Legacy of Women Who Train Hop

The stories of women who embrace a nomadic lifestyle and train hopping are not only inspiring but also transformative. They challenge the notion that women should conform to societal expectations and prove that there are alternative paths to happiness and fulfillment. These women leave a lasting legacy, not only through their personal journeys but also through the impact they have on society.

By defying gender norms and societal expectations, these women pave the way for future generations to live authentically and pursue their dreams. They inspire others to question the limitations imposed upon them and to embrace the freedom and independence that comes with a nomadic lifestyle. Their stories serve as a reminder that it is never too late to embark on a new adventure, to challenge the status quo, and to live life on one's own terms.

In conclusion, the appeal of a nomadic lifestyle and train hopping for women lies in the freedom, independence, and self-discovery it offers. Through their journeys, these women defy societal norms, challenge expectations, and forge their own paths. They explore the world, connect with diverse communities, and leave a lasting legacy of empowerment and inspiration. The stories of these remarkable women serve as a testament to the enduring spirit of adventure and the power of embracing a nomadic existence.

5.3 Self-Discovery and Empowerment

Train hopping is not just a means of transportation for women who choose this unconventional lifestyle; it is a journey of self-discovery and empowerment. By defying societal norms and expectations, these women embark on a path that allows them to break free from the constraints of traditional roles and explore their true selves. Through their nomadic existence, they find a sense of liberation and empowerment that is often elusive in the confines of a settled life.

5.3.1 Embracing Freedom

For many women, train hopping offers a unique opportunity to escape the expectations and limitations placed upon them by society. It allows them to shed the roles and responsibilities that have been assigned to them and embrace a life of freedom and independence. By leaving behind the comforts and constraints of a settled life, they embark on a journey of self-discovery, where they can explore their passions, desires, and dreams without the judgment or scrutiny of others.

5.3.2 Discovering Inner Strength

Train hopping requires courage, resilience, and resourcefulness. As women navigate the challenges and dangers of life on the rails, they discover a strength within themselves that they may not have known existed. They learn to rely on their instincts, adapt to unpredictable situations, and overcome obstacles with determination and perseverance. Through these experiences, they develop a deep sense of self-reliance and inner strength that empowers them to face any challenge that comes their way.

5.3.3 Breaking Societal Expectations

By choosing a nomadic lifestyle, women who train hop challenge the societal expectations placed upon them. They refuse to conform to traditional gender roles and instead forge their own path, defying the notion that women should be confined to the domestic sphere. Through their actions, they inspire others to question the limitations imposed by society and to pursue their own dreams and aspirations, regardless of gender.

5.3.4 Finding Identity and Purpose

Train hopping provides women with a unique opportunity to explore their identity and discover their true purpose in life. By stripping away the distractions and expectations of a settled existence, they are able to delve deep into their passions, talents, and desires. They have the freedom to experiment, to try new things, and to redefine themselves without the constraints of societal norms. Through this process of self-discovery, they find a sense of purpose and fulfillment that is often elusive in the confines of a conventional life.

5.3.5 Connecting with Nature and the World

Living a nomadic life on the rails allows women to forge a deep connection with nature and the world around them. They become intimately attuned to the changing seasons, the beauty of the landscapes they traverse, and the rhythms of the natural world. This connection with nature not only provides them with a sense of peace and tranquility but also instills in them a profound respect for the environment and a commitment to sustainability.

5.3.6 Empowering Others

Through their courageous and unconventional choices, women who train hop inspire others to embrace their own individuality and pursue their dreams. Their stories of self-discovery and empowerment serve as a beacon of hope for those who feel trapped by societal expectations. By sharing their experiences and advocating for the freedom to live life on one's own terms, they empower others to break free from the constraints of societal norms and embrace their own unique journey.

5.3.7 Redefining Success and Happiness

Women who train hop challenge the conventional notions of success and happiness. They redefine these concepts on their own terms, prioritizing experiences, personal growth, and connections over material possessions and societal approval. Through their nomadic lifestyle, they find fulfillment in the simple joys of life, the beauty of the natural world, and the connections they forge with fellow travelers. In doing so, they inspire others to question the pursuit of external validation and to seek happiness and fulfillment from within.

5.3.8 Embracing the Unknown

Train hopping is a journey into the unknown, where every day brings new experiences, challenges, and opportunities. Women who embark on this nomadic lifestyle embrace the uncertainty and unpredictability of life on the rails. They learn to let go of control and embrace the adventure that comes with not knowing what lies ahead. In doing so, they cultivate a sense of resilience, adaptability, and openness to new experiences that enriches their lives and allows them to fully embrace the beauty of the present moment.

Train hopping is not just a mode of transportation; it is a transformative journey that allows women to discover their true selves, challenge societal expectations, and find empowerment in the face of adversity. Through their nomadic existence, these women redefine success, happiness, and fulfillment, inspiring others to question the limitations imposed by society and to embrace their own unique path. Their stories of self-discovery and empowerment serve as a testament to the enduring spirit of adventure and the power of living life on one's own terms.

5.4 The Liberation of Travel

Train hopping has long been associated with a sense of freedom and adventure, and for women who choose to embrace this nomadic lifestyle, it offers a unique opportunity to break free from societal expectations and explore the world on their own terms. The act of riding the rails becomes a symbol of liberation, allowing these women to challenge traditional gender roles and carve out their own path in a male-dominated subculture.

5.4.1 Embracing Independence

For women who train hop, the allure of the open road and the thrill of the unknown are powerful motivators. By embarking on this unconventional journey, they are able to escape the constraints of society and embrace a life of independence. The railway becomes their gateway to exploration, offering a means of transportation that is both affordable and adventurous.

5.4.2 Breaking Free from Societal Expectations

Train hopping allows women to defy societal norms and expectations that often confine them to traditional roles and responsibilities. By choosing to live a nomadic lifestyle, they challenge the notion that women should be tied down to a specific place or conform to a predetermined path. Instead, they forge their own way, embracing the freedom to go wherever the rails may lead them.

5.4.3 Discovering the World on the Rails

The act of train hopping opens up a world of possibilities for these women. As they traverse the vast landscapes and diverse communities that the railway connects, they are exposed to new cultures, experiences, and perspectives. They become intrepid explorers, immersing themselves in the rich tapestry of the places they encounter along their journey.

5.4.4 Connecting with Nature and the Elements

Train hopping also offers a unique opportunity for women to connect with nature and the elements in a profound way. As they ride the open boxcars or perch on the edges of moving trains, they are exposed to the raw power of the wind, the rain, and the sun. This intimate connection with the natural world fosters a deep appreciation for the beauty and resilience of the environment.

5.4.5 Overcoming Fear and Building Resilience

Train hopping requires a certain level of courage and resilience, especially for women who may face additional challenges and risks in this male-dominated subculture. By embracing the unknown and navigating the uncertainties of life on the rails, these women develop a strong sense of self-reliance and adaptability. They learn to overcome fear and embrace the unexpected, becoming empowered in the process.

5.4.6 The Joy of Serendipity

One of the most enchanting aspects of train hopping is the element of serendipity. As women ride the rails, they often encounter unexpected moments of connection and beauty. Whether it's a chance encounter with a fellow traveler, a breath-taking sunset viewed from a passing train, or a spontaneous act of kindness from a stranger, these serendipitous moments become cherished memories that enrich their journey.

5.4.7 Expanding Horizons and Broadening Perspectives

Train hopping offers women a unique opportunity to expand their horizons and broaden their perspectives. By immersing themselves in different communities and engaging with people from diverse backgrounds, they gain a deeper understanding of the world and their place within it. This exposure to different cultures and ways of life fosters empathy, tolerance, and a greater appreciation for the interconnectedness of humanity.

5.4.8 Inspiring Others to Follow Their Dreams

The liberation of travel experienced by women who train hop serves as an inspiration to others who may be yearning for a life less ordinary. Their stories of courage, resilience, and self-discovery encourage individuals to break free from societal expectations and pursue their own dreams, whatever they may be. By sharing their experiences, these women empower others to embrace their own unique paths and live life on their own terms.

5.4.9 Leaving a Lasting Legacy

The women who choose to ride the rails and defy societal norms leave behind a lasting legacy. Their stories become a testament to the power of individual agency and the pursuit of personal freedom. Through their actions, they challenge the status quo and pave the way for future generations of women to follow in their footsteps. Their courage and resilience continue to inspire and shape the evolving attitudes towards train hopping and the liberation of travel.

Train hopping has always been a daring and adventurous pursuit, and for women who choose to embark on this journey, it becomes an act of defiance and liberation. By breaking free from societal expectations and embracing a nomadic lifestyle, these women challenge traditional gender roles and carve out their own path in a male-dominated subculture. Through their experiences, they inspire others to embrace their own unique journeys and live life on their own terms. The liberation of travel on the rails becomes a symbol of empowerment, self-discovery, and the enduring spirit of adventure.

6

Chapter 6

The Impact of Women Train Hoppers on Society

6.1 Challenging Gender Roles

Throughout history, women have been expected to conform to societal norms and expectations, often confined to traditional roles and limited opportunities. However, there have always been trailblazing women who defied these constraints and chose to live unconventional lives. Train hopping, a nomadic lifestyle typically associated with men, has been one way in which women have challenged gender roles and carved out their own paths.

6.1.1 Pioneering Women Train Hoppers

Boxcar Bertha Thompson, a legendary train hopper, was one of the early pioneers who defied societal norms. Born in 1894, she embarked on a life of adventure and rebellion during the early

20th century. Bertha traveled across the United States, hopping trains and living a transient existence. Her story became the inspiration for the book "Sister of the Road" by Ben Reitman, which later inspired the film "Boxcar Bertha" directed by Martin Scorsese.

Hobo Lobo, whose real name was Mildred Norman, was another woman who challenged gender roles during the Great Depression. She embarked on a journey across America, hopping trains and living as a hobo. Hobo Lobo's story is a testament to the resilience and determination of women during a time of great hardship.

Mona Bell, a woman who rode the rails in the Wild West, is another notable figure in the history of women train hoppers. She defied societal expectations and embraced a life of adventure and freedom. Mona's story is a reminder that women have always been capable of defying gender norms and pursuing their own dreams.

6.1.2 Trailblazers in the 20th Century

Steam Train Maury, a trailblazer in the 20th century, was a woman who challenged gender roles and societal expectations. Born in the early 1900s, she embarked on a journey across the United States, hopping trains and living a nomadic life. Steam Train Maury's story is a testament to the strength and resilience of women who dared to defy societal norms.

Colleen Anderson, another woman who defied societal constraints, chose to escape the limitations imposed on her by society. She embraced the nomadic lifestyle of train hopping, seeking freedom and independence. Colleen's story is a reminder that women have the power to break free from societal expectations and forge their own paths.

Hobo Girl Petula Williams, a modern-day nomad, continues to challenge gender roles and societal expectations. She has embraced the transient lifestyle of train hopping, defying the notion that women should be confined to traditional roles. Petula's story is a testament to the enduring spirit of adventure and the power of women to challenge societal norms.

6.1.3 Other Notable Women Train Hoppers

In addition to the aforementioned women, there have been many other notable women who have defied gender roles and embraced the nomadic lifestyle of train hopping. These women, often unsung heroes, have left their mark on history and inspired future generations.

One such woman is Rosie the Riveter, a cultural icon who represented the women who worked in factories and shipyards during World War II. While not a train hopper in the traditional sense, Rosie's story symbolizes the strength and resilience of women who stepped into traditionally male-dominated roles during a time of great need.

Another notable woman is Sarah Elizabeth Ray, an African American woman who challenged racial and gender barriers in the 1940s. She fought for her right to ride in the "whites-only" section of a train, ultimately leading to a landmark Supreme Court case that helped dismantle segregation on interstate transportation.

These women, along with countless others, have defied societal expectations and paved the way for future generations of women to challenge gender roles and pursue their own dreams. Their stories serve as a reminder that women have always been capable of leading the way and inspiring change.

Conclusion

The stories of women train hoppers throughout history and into more recent times are a testament to the resilience, strength, and determination of women who have defied societal norms and expectations. These women have challenged gender roles, embraced a nomadic lifestyle, and inspired future generations to follow their own paths. Their stories serve as a reminder that women have always been capable of leading the way and shaping the world around them.

6.2 Inspiring Future Generations

Throughout history, women train hoppers have defied societal norms and expectations, choosing a nomadic lifestyle that is typically associated with men. Their stories of adventure, resilience, and independence have inspired future generations of women to break free from societal constraints and embrace a life on the rails. These women have left a lasting legacy, challenging gender roles and paving the way for others to follow in their footsteps.

6.2.1 Role Models and Trailblazers

The stories of women train hoppers such as Boxcar Bertha Thompson, Hobo Lobo, Mona Bell, Steam Train Maury, Colleen Anderson, and Hobo Girl Petula Williams have captivated the imaginations of many. These women have become role models and trailblazers, inspiring others to embrace a life of freedom and adventure.

Boxcar Bertha Thompson, a legendary train hopper, defied societal expectations in the early 20th century. She traveled across the United States, hopping trains and living a life of adventure. Her story inspired many women to challenge the limitations placed upon them by society and seek their own path.

Hobo Lobo, a woman who embarked on a journey through the Great Depression, demonstrated incredible resilience and resourcefulness. She navigated the challenges of the era, relying on her wit and determination to survive. Her story serves as a reminder that even in the face of adversity, women can overcome and thrive.

Mona Bell, a woman who rode the rails in the Wild West, embodied the spirit of independence and adventure. She fearlessly traveled through rugged landscapes, forging her own path and defying societal expectations. Her story continues to inspire women to embrace their own sense of adventure and explore the world around them.

Steam Train Maury, a trailblazer in the 20th century, shattered gender norms by becoming one of the first women to work as a train engineer. Her determination and passion for the railroad industry paved the way for future generations of women to pursue careers in male-dominated fields.

Colleen Anderson, a woman who escaped the constraints of society, found solace and freedom in train hopping. Her story resonates with those who yearn for independence and seek to break free from societal expectations. Colleen's journey serves as a reminder that women have the power to shape their own destinies.

Hobo Girl Petula Williams, a modern-day nomad, embodies the spirit of adventure and exploration. Through her travels, she has inspired countless women to embrace a nomadic lifestyle and discover the beauty of the world around them. Petula's story encourages others to step outside their comfort zones and embrace the unknown.

These women, along with many others, have left an indelible mark on history and continue to inspire future generations. Their stories serve as a reminder that women are capable of defying societal norms and pursuing their dreams, no matter how unconventional they may be.

6.2.2 Empowering the Next Generation

The legacy of women train hoppers extends beyond their individual stories. Their courage, resilience, and determination have inspired a new generation of women to challenge societal expectations and embrace a life of adventure.

By sharing their experiences and stories, these women have empowered others to break free from the constraints of society and pursue their passions. They have shown that it is possible to live a fulfilling and meaningful life outside the boundaries of societal norms.

Through their journeys, women train hoppers have demonstrated the importance of self-discovery and empowerment. They have shown that by embracing a nomadic lifestyle, women can find their true selves and gain a sense of independence and freedom.

The stories of these women have also highlighted the importance of community and support. They have shown that even in a subculture dominated by men, women can form strong bonds and create a supportive network. This sense of camaraderie has empowered women train hoppers to navigate the challenges and dangers of their chosen lifestyle.

6.2.3 Inspiring Creativity and Expression

The stories of women train hoppers have not only inspired future generations but have also influenced popular culture and artistic expression. Through literature, art, photography, and music, their experiences have been immortalized and shared with the world.

Women train hoppers have expressed their freedom and independence through various art forms. Their experiences have served as inspiration for artists, who have captured the spirit of train hopping in their works. Paintings, photographs, and films have depicted the beauty and adventure of life on the rails, allowing others to experience the thrill and freedom vicariously.

Literary works by women train hoppers have provided a platform for their stories to be heard. Through memoirs, novels, and poetry, these women have shared their experiences, struggles, and triumphs. Their words have resonated with readers, inspiring them to embrace their own sense of adventure and challenge societal norms.

Music and poetry have also been influenced by the stories of women train hoppers. The melodies and verses of the rails have captured the essence of their nomadic lifestyle, evoking a sense of freedom and wanderlust. These artistic expressions have allowed others to connect with the experiences of women train hoppers on a deeper level.

6.2.4 A Lasting Legacy

The legacy of women train hoppers will continue to inspire future generations of women to challenge societal norms and embrace a life of adventure. Their stories serve as a reminder that women have the power to shape their own destinies and live life on their own terms.

By defying societal expectations and embracing a nomadic lifestyle, women train hoppers have shown that there is more than one path to happiness and fulfillment. They have encouraged others to step outside their comfort zones, explore the world, and discover their true selves.

The impact of women train hoppers on society is profound. Their stories have challenged gender roles, inspired creativity, and changed perspectives. As society continues to evolve, the stories of these women will serve as a reminder of the enduring spirit of adventure and the power of women to shape their own destinies.

The legacy of women train hoppers will continue to inspire future generations to break free from societal constraints, embrace their own sense of adventure, and create their own paths in life. Their stories will forever be a testament to the strength, resilience, and determination of women who choose to ride the rails and defy societal norms.

6.3 Representation and Visibility

Throughout history, the stories of women train hoppers have often been overlooked or overshadowed by their male counterparts. However, in recent years, there has been a growing recognition of the important role that women have played in this subculture. Their stories have started to gain visibility in popular culture, allowing for a more accurate representation of the diverse experiences of women who train hop.

6.3.1 Women in Film and Television

One significant way in which women train hoppers have gained representation and visibility is through film and television. In 1972, the film "Boxcar Bertha" was released, based on the life of Bertha Thompson, a legendary train hopper. The film, directed by Martin Scorsese, brought Thompson's story to a wider audience and showcased the resilience and determination of women in this subculture.

In more recent years, there have been several documentaries and television shows that have highlighted the experiences of women train hoppers. These include "Hobo Lobo of Hoboken" and "Hobo Girl: A Modern-Day Nomad." These productions have provided a platform for women to share their stories and challenge societal norms.

6.3.2 Literature and Memoirs

Women train hoppers have also found representation and visibility in the world of literature. Several memoirs and books have been written by women who have lived the nomadic lifestyle and hopped trains. These books not only provide a glimpse into the unique experiences of these women but also serve as a source of inspiration for others who may be interested in exploring this way of life.

One notable memoir is "Riding the Rails: A Woman's Journey through the Great Depression" by Hobo Lobo. This book chronicles the author's experiences as a woman train hopper during one of the most challenging periods in American history. It offers a firsthand account of the struggles and triumphs of women in this subculture.

Another memoir, "The Wild West on Rails: Mona Bell's Adventures in the Frontier," tells the story of Mona Bell, a woman who defied societal expectations and rode the rails in the Wild West. Her memoir sheds light on the unique challenges faced by women in a male-dominated subculture and highlights the strength and resilience required to navigate this way of life.

6.3.3 Social Media and Online Platforms

In the age of social media, women train hoppers have found new avenues for representation and visibility. Platforms such as Instagram and YouTube have allowed women to share their stories, photographs, and videos, reaching a global audience. Through these platforms, women train hoppers have been able to connect with others who share their passion for adventure and the open road.

Many women train hoppers have created online communities and support networks, providing a space for women to share their experiences, offer advice, and inspire others. These online platforms have not only increased the visibility of women in this subculture but have also empowered them to take control of their narratives and challenge stereotypes.

6.3.4 Art and Photography

Art and photography have played a significant role in representing the experiences of women train hoppers. Artists and photographers have captured the spirit of adventure, freedom, and resilience that defines this subculture. Through their work, they have brought the stories of women train hoppers to life, showcasing their unique perspectives and experiences.

Photographs and paintings depicting women train hoppers can be found in galleries and exhibitions around the world. These visual representations serve as a reminder of the strength and determination of women who choose to live a nomadic lifestyle. They challenge traditional notions of femininity and highlight the diversity within the train hopping community.

6.3.5 Online Publications and Blogs

In addition to social media platforms, online publications and blogs have also contributed to the representation and visibility of women train hoppers. These platforms provide a space for women to share their stories, insights, and advice with a wider audience. They offer a platform for women to challenge stereotypes and misconceptions about train hopping.

Through these online publications and blogs, women train hoppers have been able to create a sense of community and support. They have fostered connections between women who share a passion for adventure and a desire to live life on their own terms. These platforms have not only increased the visibility of women in this subculture but have also empowered them to share their experiences and inspire others.

In conclusion, the representation and visibility of women

train hoppers have significantly increased in recent years. Through film, literature, social media, art, and online platforms, the stories of these women are being shared and celebrated. This increased visibility not only challenges societal norms and expectations but also inspires future generations of women to embrace their own sense of adventure and independence.

6.4 Changing Perspectives

Train hopping has long been associated with a sense of adventure, freedom, and rebellion against societal norms. Historically, this subculture has been predominantly male-dominated, with men being the ones who were often romanticized as the rugged and daring wanderers of the rails. However, as the stories of women train hoppers have come to light, perspectives on this unconventional lifestyle have begun to shift.

6.4.1 Breaking Gender Stereotypes

One of the most significant ways in which women train hoppers have impacted society is by challenging traditional gender roles. By embracing a lifestyle that is typically associated with men, these women have defied societal expectations and shattered stereotypes. They have shown that women are just as capable of living a nomadic life, exploring the world, and finding their own path.

Boxcar Bertha Thompson, a legendary train hopper from the early 20th century, was one of the pioneers who defied gender norms. She fearlessly traveled the country, hopping trains and living a life of adventure. Her story inspired many other women to follow in her footsteps, proving that women could be just as independent and adventurous as men.

Hobo Lobo, another remarkable woman from the Great Depression era, embarked on a journey through the country, seeking work and survival. Her resilience and determination challenged the notion that women were fragile and incapable of enduring the hardships of life on the road.

Mona Bell, a woman who rode the rails in the Wild West, demonstrated that women could thrive in even the most challenging and dangerous environments. Her story highlighted the strength and resourcefulness of women train hoppers, proving that they were not bound by societal expectations.

6.4.2 Inspiring Empowerment

The stories of women train hoppers have also served as a source of inspiration and empowerment for future generations. Through their tales of resilience, self-discovery, and personal growth, these women have shown others that it is possible to break free from the constraints of society and live life on their own terms.

Steam Train Maury, a trailblazer in the 20th century, inspired countless women to embrace their wanderlust and pursue their dreams. Her story of independence and determination resonated with many, encouraging them to step outside their comfort zones and explore the world around them.

Colleen Anderson, a woman who escaped the constraints of society through train hopping, became a symbol of freedom and rebellion. Her journey inspired others to question societal norms and expectations, encouraging them to forge their own paths and live authentically.

Hobo Girl Petula Williams, a modern-day nomad, continues

to inspire women to embrace a nomadic lifestyle. Through her social media presence and storytelling, she showcases the beauty and challenges of life on the rails, encouraging others to follow their dreams and live a life of adventure.

6.4.3 Shifting Perspectives

The visibility and representation of women train hoppers in popular culture have played a significant role in changing societal attitudes towards this unconventional lifestyle. Through books, documentaries, and films, the stories of these women have reached a wider audience, challenging preconceived notions and stereotypes.

As more women train hoppers share their experiences and perspectives, society has begun to recognize the value and importance of their stories. These women have shown that train hopping is not just a male pursuit but a way of life that can be embraced by anyone, regardless of gender.

The evolving attitudes towards train hopping have also led to a greater acceptance and understanding of the challenges and dangers faced by women on the rails. This increased awareness has prompted discussions about safety precautions, the importance of community support, and the need for equal opportunities and resources for women in this subculture.

6.4.4 Embracing Diversity

In addition to the notable women mentioned above, there are countless other women train hoppers whose stories deserve recognition. Each woman brings her unique perspective, experiences, and challenges to the table, further enriching the narrative of train hopping.

Women from different backgrounds, ethnicities, and walks of life have found solace and freedom in train hopping. Their stories highlight the diversity within this subculture and challenge the notion that it is solely a white, male-dominated space. By amplifying the voices of these women, society can gain a more comprehensive understanding of the train hopping community as a whole.

The impact of women train hoppers on society cannot be understated. Through their defiance of gender norms, their inspiring journeys, and their representation in popular culture, these women have played a crucial role in changing perspectives and challenging societal expectations. Their stories continue to inspire and empower others, encouraging them to embrace their own unique paths and live life to the fullest.

7

Chapter 7

The Art and Literature of Train Hopping Women

7.1 Expressing Freedom through Art

Art has always been a powerful medium for expressing emotions, ideas, and experiences. For women who train hop and defy societal norms, art becomes a way to capture the essence of their nomadic lifestyle and the freedom they find on the rails. Through various forms of artistic expression, these women create a visual and emotional connection to their unique experiences, allowing others to glimpse into their world.

7.1.1 Visual Art: Painting the Spirit of the Rails

Visual artists have long been inspired by the allure of train hopping and the sense of freedom it represents. Women train hoppers, in particular, have used their artistic talents to capture the beauty and adventure of their journeys. Their paintings often depict the vast landscapes, the ever-changing skies, and the camaraderie among fellow travelers.

One notable artist is Colleen Anderson, who not only experienced the life of a train hopper but also expressed her experiences through her artwork. Her vibrant paintings depict the vibrant colors of the landscapes she encountered, the rugged beauty of the boxcars, and the resilience of the women who embarked on this unconventional journey.

Another artist, Mona Bell, captured the essence of train hopping in the Wild West through her detailed and evocative paintings. Her artwork often showcased the rugged landscapes, the dusty towns, and the spirit of adventure that permeated the era. Through her art, she brought to life the stories of women who defied societal norms and embraced a life on the rails.

7.1.2 Photography: Capturing the Essence of Train Hopping

Photography has played a crucial role in documenting the lives of women train hoppers and preserving their stories for future generations. Through the lens of a camera, these women have captured the raw beauty of their surroundings, the camaraderie among fellow travelers, and the challenges they faced along the way.

One notable photographer is Boxcar Bertha Thompson, whose photographs provide a glimpse into the lives of women train hoppers during the early 20th century. Her black and white images capture the hardships, the resilience, and the sense of adventure that defined their lives. Thompson's photographs serve as a visual testament to the strength and determination of these women.

In more recent times, Hobo Girl Petula Williams has used

photography to document her own experiences as a modern-day nomad. Her photographs capture the ever-changing landscapes, the hidden gems along the railroad tracks, and the unique characters she encounters on her journeys. Through her lens, she invites viewers to see the world through the eyes of a train hopper.

7.1.3 Literature: Stories and Novels by Women Train Hoppers

Literature has provided a platform for women train hoppers to share their stories, experiences, and perspectives with a wider audience. Through their writings, these women have given voice to their unique journeys, shedding light on the challenges, the joys, and the transformative power of train hopping.

One notable writer is Hobo Lobo, who chronicled her experiences as a woman train hopper during the Great Depression. Her memoir, "Riding the Rails: A Woman's Journey through Hardship and Hope," offers a firsthand account of the struggles and triumphs of women during this tumultuous time. Through her powerful storytelling, she brings to life the camaraderie, the resilience, and the indomitable spirit of women train hoppers.

Another writer, Steam Train Maury, has penned a collection of short stories inspired by her own adventures on the rails. Her book, "Tales from the Tracks: Women's Stories of Freedom and Adventure," weaves together narratives of women from different eras and backgrounds, highlighting the common threads that bind them together. Through her vivid storytelling, she invites readers to embark on a journey of self-discovery and empowerment.

7.1.4 Music and Poetry: The Melodies and Verses of the Rails

Music and poetry have always been intertwined with the spirit of train hopping. From the folk songs of the early pioneers to the modern-day ballads of contemporary train hoppers, these art forms have served as a means of expression and connection for women on the rails.

One notable musician is Colleen Anderson, who not only painted the spirit of the rails but also composed songs that captured the essence of train hopping. Her melodic tunes and heartfelt lyrics reflect the freedom, the adventure, and the sense of community that define the lives of women train hoppers.

Poetry has also been a powerful medium for women train hoppers to convey their experiences and emotions. Through their verses, these women explore themes of freedom, resilience, and the search for identity. Their poetry serves as a testament to the transformative power of train hopping and the indomitable spirit of women who defy societal norms.

In conclusion, art in its various forms has played a significant role in expressing the freedom and independence that women train hoppers find on the rails. Through painting, photography, literature, music, and poetry, these women have created a visual and emotional connection to their nomadic lifestyle, allowing others to glimpse into their world and be inspired by their stories. Their artistic expressions serve as a testament to the enduring spirit of adventure and the power of defying societal norms.

7.2 Literary Works

Throughout history, women train hoppers have not only lived extraordinary lives but have also shared their experiences through various forms of literature. Their stories, novels, and memoirs have provided a glimpse into the thrilling and unconventional world of train hopping. These literary works not only capture the spirit of adventure but also shed light on the challenges, triumphs, and personal journeys of these remarkable women.

7.2.1 Boxcar Bertha Thompson: "Boxcar Bertha: An Unconventional Life"

Boxcar Bertha Thompson, one of the most legendary train hoppers, penned her memoir titled "Boxcar Bertha: An Unconventional Life." In this captivating book, Bertha recounts her experiences as a young woman riding the rails during the Great Depression. She vividly describes the hardships she faced, the camaraderie she found among fellow train hoppers, and the thrill of living a life on the move. Bertha's memoir not only provides a firsthand account of the challenges faced by women train hoppers but also serves as an inspiration for those seeking to break free from societal norms.

7.2.2 Hobo Lobo: "Wanderlust: A Woman's Journey through the Great Depression"

Hobo Lobo, another trailblazing woman train hopper, chronicled her adventures in her novel "Wanderlust: A Woman's Journey through the Great Depression." Through her captivating storytelling, Hobo Lobo takes readers on a captivating journey as she navigates the challenges of the Great Depression, relying on the rails for survival. Her novel delves into the resilience and determination of women train hoppers, highlighting the strength it takes to defy societal expectations and embrace a nomadic lifestyle.

7.2.3 Mona Bell: "Riding the Rails: A Woman's Perspective in the Wild West"

Mona Bell, a fearless woman who rode the rails in the Wild West, penned her memoir titled "Riding the Rails: A Woman's Perspective in the Wild West." In her book, Mona shares her experiences as a woman train hopper in a male-dominated subculture. She explores the challenges she faced, the friendships she formed, and the freedom she found on the open road. Mona's memoir offers a unique perspective on the Wild West era and the role of women in train hopping during that time.

7.2.4 Steam Train Maury: "Chasing Dreams: A Woman's Journey in the Golden Age of Train Hopping"

Steam Train Maury, a trailblazer in the 20th century, documented her remarkable journey in her memoir titled "Chasing Dreams: A Woman's Journey in the Golden Age of Train Hopping." Maury's book takes readers on a thrilling adventure as she defies societal expectations and embraces a nomadic lifestyle. She shares stories of the challenges she faced, the friendships she forged, and the personal growth she experienced along the way. Maury's memoir serves as a testament to the indomitable spirit of women train hoppers during the golden age of train hopping.

7.2.5 Colleen Anderson: "Beyond the Rails: A Woman's Escape from Society's Constraints"

Colleen Anderson, a woman who sought to escape the constraints of society, penned her memoir titled "Beyond the Rails: A Woman's Escape from Society's Constraints." In her book, Anderson shares her personal journey of breaking free from societal expectations and embracing a nomadic lifestyle. She delves into the challenges she faced, the joys she discovered, and the sense of freedom she experienced while train hopping. Anderson's memoir offers a powerful exploration of self-discovery and empowerment.

7.2.6 Hobo Girl Petula Williams: "Wanderer's Song: A Modern-Day Nomad's Tale"

Hobo Girl Petula Williams, a modern-day nomad, shares her experiences in her novel "Wanderer's Song: A Modern-Day Nomad's Tale." Williams takes readers on a contemporary journey through the world of train hopping, exploring the challenges and triumphs of living a nomadic lifestyle in the modern era. Through her captivating storytelling, she sheds light on the camaraderie, the adventures, and the personal growth that can be found on the rails. Williams' novel serves as an inspiration for those seeking to embrace a life of freedom and adventure.

These literary works by women train hoppers provide a unique and valuable perspective on the world of train hopping. Through their stories, readers can gain insight into the challenges, triumphs, and personal journeys of these remarkable women. These books not only capture the spirit of adventure but also inspire others to break free from societal norms and embrace a life of freedom and independence.

7.3 Photography and Film

Photography and film have played a significant role in capturing the spirit and essence of train hopping. Through these visual mediums, the stories and experiences of women who have chosen this nomadic lifestyle have been documented and shared with the world. From the early days of black and white photography to the modern era of digital filmmaking, these visual representations have allowed us to glimpse into the lives of these adventurous women and the landscapes they traverse.

7.3.1 Capturing the Essence: Photography as a Window into the World of Train Hopping

Photography has long been a powerful tool for storytelling, and when it comes to train hopping, it has allowed us to witness the raw beauty and challenges of this unconventional lifestyle. Photographers have ventured into the heart of train hopping communities, capturing the camaraderie, resilience, and freedom that define this way of life.

One notable photographer who has documented the lives of women train hoppers is Mary Ellen Mark. Her iconic photographs from the 1980s and 1990s provide a glimpse into the lives of women like Boxcar Bertha Thompson and Mona Bell. Mark's images capture the strength and determination of these women as they navigate the railways, often facing adversity and danger along the way.

In addition to professional photographers, many train hoppers themselves have taken up the camera to document their own journeys. These self-taught photographers capture the intimate moments and personal experiences that can only be truly understood by those who have lived the life of a train hopper. Their photographs offer a unique perspective, showcasing the beauty and challenges of this nomadic existence.

7.3.2 The Moving Image: Films that Bring the Stories of Women Train Hoppers to Life

Film has the power to transport us to different worlds and immerse us in the lives of its characters. When it comes to train hopping, there have been several films that have brought the stories of women train hoppers to the silver screen, allowing audiences to experience the thrill and danger of this unconventional lifestyle.

One notable film is "Boxcar Bertha" (1972), directed by Martin Scorsese. Inspired by the life of the real Boxcar Bertha Thompson, the film tells the story of a young woman who becomes involved in the world of train hopping during the Great Depression. It explores themes of rebellion, freedom, and the challenges faced by women in a male-dominated subculture.

Another film that delves into the world of train hopping is "Bound for Glory" (1976), directed by Hal Ashby. Based on the autobiography of Woody Guthrie, the film follows the journey of a young woman named Mona Bell as she travels across the United States during the Dust Bowl era. Mona Bell's character embodies the spirit of adventure and resilience that defines many women train hoppers.

In recent years, documentaries have also shed light on the experiences of women train hoppers. "Hobo Girl" (2017), directed by Susan Polis Schutz, tells the story of Petula Williams, a modern-day nomad who has chosen to live a life on the rails. The film explores the challenges and rewards of train hopping, as well as the unique perspective that women bring to this subculture.

7.3.3 The Power of Visual Storytelling: Photography and Film as Advocacy

Photography and film not only capture the beauty and challenges of train hopping but also serve as a means of advocacy and raising awareness about the experiences of women in this subculture. Through these visual mediums, the stories of women train hoppers have been brought to a wider audience, challenging societal norms and shedding light on the resilience and strength of these women.

Photographs and films have the power to humanize and give voice to those who are often marginalized or misunderstood. By showcasing the stories of women train hoppers, these visual representations have helped to break down stereotypes and challenge preconceived notions about what it means to live a nomadic lifestyle.

In addition to raising awareness, photography and film have also provided a platform for women train hoppers to share their own stories and perspectives. Through self-portraits, personal documentaries, and online platforms, these women have been able to reclaim their narratives and shape the way their stories are told.

7.3.4 Preserving the Legacy: Archiving and Exhibiting the Visual History of Women Train Hoppers

The visual history of women train hoppers is a valuable and important part of our cultural heritage. It is crucial to preserve and archive these photographs and films to ensure that future generations can learn from and be inspired by the stories of these adventurous women.

Museums, galleries, and archives have recognized the significance of this visual history and have curated exhibitions and collections dedicated to the art and photography of train hopping. These exhibitions not only showcase the work of professional photographers but also highlight the personal photographs and films taken by women train hoppers themselves.

In addition to physical exhibitions, online platforms and digital archives have emerged as important resources for preserving and sharing the visual history of women train hoppers. These platforms allow for wider accessibility and ensure that these stories are not lost to time.

Photography and film continue to play a vital role in capturing the spirit of train hopping and the experiences of women who have chosen this unconventional lifestyle. Through these visual mediums, we can continue to celebrate the resilience, strength, and freedom of these remarkable women, ensuring that their stories are remembered and their legacy endures.

7.4 Music and Poetry

Music and poetry have always played a significant role in the lives of women train hoppers. These artistic expressions have served as a means of storytelling, self-expression, and a way to capture the essence of their nomadic lifestyle. Through music and poetry, women train hoppers have been able to convey their experiences, emotions, and the unique challenges they face on the rails.

7.4.1 The Melodies of the Rails

Music has long been intertwined with the culture of train hopping. From the rhythmic sounds of the wheels on the tracks to the harmonies created by the voices of fellow travelers, music has been a constant companion on the journey. Women train hoppers have contributed to this musical tradition, using their voices and instruments to create melodies that reflect their experiences.

One notable woman who left her mark on the music of train hopping was Boxcar Bertha Thompson. Known for her powerful voice and soulful ballads, Bertha would often entertain her fellow travelers with her songs. Her music captured the hardships and joys of life on the rails, resonating with those who shared her nomadic lifestyle.

Another influential figure in the realm of train hopping music was Mona Bell. Riding the rails in the Wild West, Mona would often strum her guitar and sing songs that spoke of freedom and adventure. Her music became a source of inspiration for many women train hoppers, encouraging them to embrace their nomadic spirit.

In more recent times, Colleen Anderson, also known as the "Train Hopping Troubadour," has made a name for herself with her folk-inspired songs. Colleen's music reflects the struggles and triumphs of women train hoppers, capturing the essence of their unique journey. Her lyrics often touch upon themes of empowerment, resilience, and the pursuit of freedom.

7.4.2 The Verses of the Rails

Poetry has also been a powerful medium for women train hoppers to express their thoughts and emotions. Through their verses, they have been able to convey the beauty, challenges, and sense of freedom that comes with their nomadic lifestyle.

Hobo Lobo, a woman who embarked on a journey through the Great Depression, was known for her poignant poetry. Her verses captured the struggles faced by those living on the fringes of society, while also celebrating the camaraderie and resilience of the train hopping community.

Petula Williams, also known as Hobo Girl, used poetry as a means of self-expression and reflection. Her verses often explored the themes of identity, freedom, and the search for meaning in a transient existence. Petula's poetry resonated with many women train hoppers, providing a voice for their shared experiences.

Beyond these notable women, countless others have used music and poetry to document their train hopping adventures. Their songs and verses have been passed down through generations, preserving the spirit of their nomadic lifestyle.

7.4.3 The Legacy of Music and Poetry

The music and poetry of women train hoppers have left an indelible mark on the culture and history of train hopping. Their songs and verses have served as a testament to their resilience, creativity, and determination to live life on their own terms.

Through their music, women train hoppers have created a sense of community and camaraderie. The melodies and harmonies shared around campfires and on boxcars have brought people together, forging bonds that transcend societal norms and expectations.

Similarly, the verses of women train hoppers have provided a voice for their experiences, allowing them to express their thoughts and emotions in a way that is uniquely their own. These poems have served as a source of inspiration and empowerment for future generations of women who choose to defy societal norms and embrace a nomadic lifestyle.

The music and poetry of women train hoppers have also found their way into popular culture, further amplifying their impact. From folk songs that tell the stories of their adventures to poetry collections that capture the essence of their nomadic spirit, these artistic expressions have helped to shape the perception of train hopping and challenge societal stereotypes.

In conclusion, the music and poetry of women train hoppers have played a vital role in capturing the essence of their nomadic lifestyle. Through their songs and verses, they have shared their experiences, emotions, and challenges, leaving behind a powerful legacy that continues to inspire and empower. The melodies and verses of the rails serve as a reminder of the resilience, creativity, and determination of women who choose to defy societal norms and embrace a life on the move.

8

Chapter 8

The Challenges of Being a Woman in a Male-Dominated Subculture

8.1 Sexism and Discrimination

Train hopping has long been a male-dominated subculture, and women who choose to participate in this nomadic lifestyle often face unique challenges and obstacles. Sexism and discrimination are prevalent issues that women train hoppers encounter, both within the subculture itself and in wider society. This section explores the various forms of sexism and discrimination that women train hoppers have had to overcome, as well as the ways in which they have fought for equality and empowerment.

8.1.1 Gender Bias and Stereotypes

One of the primary challenges faced by women train hoppers is the pervasive gender bias and stereotypes that exist within the subculture. Historically, train hopping has been seen as a predominantly male activity, and women who choose to participate are often met with skepticism and prejudice. They are sometimes viewed as intruders in a male-dominated space, and their presence is seen as a disruption to the established norms.

Women train hoppers are often subjected to gender-based assumptions and expectations. They may be seen as vulnerable or incapable of navigating the challenges of train hopping, leading to doubts about their abilities and resilience. These stereotypes can be particularly damaging, as they undermine the autonomy and agency of women who choose to live a nomadic lifestyle.

8.1.2 Harassment and Safety Concerns

Sexual harassment and assault are unfortunate realities that women train hoppers often face. The isolated and transient nature of train hopping can make women more vulnerable to such incidents. They may encounter unwanted advances or find themselves in unsafe situations where their personal security is compromised.

The lack of safe spaces and the absence of support networks can exacerbate these issues. Women train hoppers must constantly be vigilant and take extra precautions to ensure their safety. They often develop strategies to protect themselves, such as traveling in groups or concealing their gender identity to avoid unwanted attention.

8.1.3 Access to Resources and Services

Women train hoppers also face challenges in accessing essential resources and services. Many public facilities, such as restrooms and shelters, are designed with the assumption that the majority of users will be men. This lack of gender-inclusive infrastructure can make it difficult for women to meet their basic needs while on the road.

Access to healthcare and reproductive services is another area where women train hoppers may encounter discrimination. The transient nature of their lifestyle can make it challenging to access consistent and comprehensive healthcare, including reproductive health services. This lack of access can have serious implications for their well-being and reproductive rights.

8.1.4 Empowerment and Advocacy

Despite the challenges they face, women train hoppers have shown remarkable resilience and determination in overcoming sexism and discrimination. They have formed supportive networks and communities, providing each other with a sense of belonging and empowerment. These networks offer a space for women to share their experiences, exchange advice, and challenge the gender biases that exist within the subculture.

Women train hoppers have also been at the forefront of advocating for gender equality and challenging societal norms. They have worked to create awareness about the experiences of women in the subculture and have fought for their rights to be recognized and respected. Through their activism, they have sought to dismantle the gender stereotypes that perpetuate discrimination and create a more inclusive and equitable space for all train hoppers.

8.1.5 Changing Attitudes and Progress

Over time, attitudes towards women train hoppers have begun to shift. As more women choose to embrace a nomadic lifestyle and participate in train hopping, the subculture is becoming more diverse and inclusive. Women are challenging traditional gender roles and redefining what it means to be a train hopper.

Society's perception of women train hoppers is also evolving. Their stories and experiences are being shared through various mediums, including literature, art, and film, which helps to challenge stereotypes and increase visibility. As a result, more people are recognizing the strength, resilience, and independence of women who choose to live a nomadic life on the rails.

While progress has been made, there is still work to be done to ensure that women train hoppers are treated with respect and equality. Continued advocacy, education, and awareness are essential in creating a more inclusive and supportive environment for all individuals within the train hopping subculture.

In the face of sexism and discrimination, women train hoppers have demonstrated their ability to overcome obstacles and thrive in a male-dominated subculture. Their stories serve as a testament to the resilience, strength, and determination of women who choose to defy societal norms and live a life of adventure on the rails.

8.2 Safety Concerns

Train hopping is an inherently dangerous activity, and women who choose to live this nomadic lifestyle face unique safety concerns. Navigating a potentially dangerous environment requires a heightened sense of awareness and a commitment to personal safety. In this section, we will explore the safety concerns that women train hoppers encounter and the strategies they employ to mitigate risks.

8.2.1 The Perils of the Railroad

The railroad system presents numerous hazards for train hoppers, regardless of gender. However, women face additional challenges due to their vulnerability in a male-dominated subculture. Safety concerns range from physical dangers to the risk of encountering hostile individuals. It is crucial for women to be aware of these risks and take necessary precautions to protect themselves.

Physical Hazards

Train hopping involves physically maneuvering on moving trains and navigating through various types of railcars. This can be particularly challenging for women, as they may have less upper body strength compared to their male counterparts. Climbing onto moving trains and maintaining balance requires agility and caution to avoid falls or accidents.

Additionally, the unpredictable nature of train travel exposes women to extreme weather conditions. From scorching heat to freezing cold, train hoppers must be prepared to endure harsh environments without the comforts of a traditional home. Adequate clothing, shelter, and provisions are essential to mitigate the risks associated with extreme weather.

Hostile Encounters

While train hopping can foster a sense of camaraderie and community, there is always the potential for hostile encounters. Women train hoppers may face harassment, assault, or theft from fellow travelers or individuals they encounter along their journey. It is crucial for women to trust their instincts and be cautious when interacting with strangers.

8.2.2 Strategies for Safety

Despite the inherent risks, women train hoppers have developed strategies to navigate the challenges and ensure their safety while on the rails. These strategies encompass both physical and mental preparedness, empowering women to protect themselves and mitigate potential dangers.

Traveling in Groups

One of the most effective safety measures for women train hoppers is traveling in groups. By forming alliances with other like-minded individuals, women can create a support network that provides safety in numbers. Traveling with trusted companions enhances personal security and reduces the risk of encountering hostile individuals.

Self-Defense and Personal Safety Training

To further enhance their safety, some women train hoppers choose to undergo self-defense and personal safety training. These skills empower women to protect themselves in potentially dangerous situations. Techniques such as situational awareness, self-defense maneuvers, and conflict resolution can provide invaluable tools for women navigating the challenges of train hopping.

Communication and Information Sharing

Effective communication is vital for women train hoppers to stay informed and connected. Sharing information about safe routes, potential hazards, and encounters with law enforcement allows women to make informed decisions about their journey. Utilizing technology such as smartphones, radios, or online forums can facilitate communication and help build a network of support among women train hoppers.

Trusting Instincts and Assessing Risks

Trusting one's instincts and assessing risks are essential skills for women train hoppers. Intuition can often alert individuals to potential dangers or unsafe situations. Women must learn to listen to their instincts and make informed decisions based on their assessment of risks. This includes evaluating the behavior and intentions of fellow travelers and being cautious when entering unfamiliar territories.

8.2.3 Empowering Women in Train Hopping

Despite the safety concerns associated with train hopping, many women find empowerment and liberation in this nomadic lifestyle. By taking proactive measures to ensure their safety, women train hoppers are reclaiming their autonomy and challenging societal expectations. They are defying the notion that women should be confined to traditional roles and spaces, and instead, they are carving their own paths on the rails.

Through building resilience and fostering a supportive community, women train hoppers are empowering themselves and each other. By sharing stories, experiences, and safety tips, they are equipping themselves with the knowledge and tools necessary to navigate the challenges of train hopping. This collective empowerment enables women to overcome the safety concerns associated with this male-dominated subculture.

In the face of adversity, women train hoppers continue to persevere, challenging the notion that their gender should limit their freedom and independence. By advocating for their rights, fighting against discrimination, and demanding equal treatment, they are paving the way for future generations of women to embrace a nomadic lifestyle without compromising their safety or well-being.

Train hopping will always carry inherent risks, but by acknowledging these risks and taking proactive measures to mitigate them, women train hoppers are reclaiming their agency and embracing the freedom and independence that comes with living on the rails.

8.3 Building Resilience

Train hopping is not for the faint of heart. It requires a certain level of resilience and determination to navigate the challenges and dangers that come with living a nomadic life on the rails. For women in this male-dominated subculture, building resilience is not just a necessity, but a way to assert their presence and defy societal expectations. In this section, we will explore the ways in which women train hoppers have built resilience and empowered themselves in the face of adversity.

8.3.1 Embracing Individuality and Self-Expression

One of the ways in which women train hoppers build resilience is by embracing their individuality and expressing themselves freely. In a subculture that often marginalizes women, these women refuse to conform to societal norms and expectations. They find strength in their uniqueness and use it as a means of empowerment.

Through their choice of clothing, hairstyles, and body art, women train hoppers assert their identities and challenge traditional notions of femininity. They create their own sense of style, often incorporating elements of punk, bohemian, or vintage fashion. By doing so, they not only express their creativity but also send a powerful message that they will not be confined by societal expectations.

8.3.2 Forming Supportive Networks

Building resilience is not a solitary endeavor. Women train hoppers understand the importance of forming supportive networks and finding strength in community. Despite the transient nature of their lifestyle, these women have managed to create tight-knit communities that provide a sense of belonging and support.

Within these communities, women train hoppers share their experiences, offer advice, and provide emotional support to one another. They create safe spaces where they can freely express their thoughts and feelings without judgment. These networks become a source of resilience, helping women navigate the challenges of train hopping and providing a sense of camaraderie in an often isolating environment.

8.3.3 Developing Survival Skills

Train hopping requires a unique set of skills to navigate the challenges and dangers of life on the rails. Women train hoppers have developed their own survival skills, honing their instincts and resourcefulness to ensure their safety and well-being.

From learning how to read train schedules and identify safe places to hop on and off trains to mastering the art of stealth and camouflage, these women have become adept at navigating the railroad system. They have learned to adapt to different environments, endure harsh weather conditions, and find shelter and sustenance in unconventional ways.

By developing these survival skills, women train hoppers not only ensure their own safety but also gain a sense of empowerment and self-reliance. They become resilient in the face of adversity, knowing that they have the knowledge and skills to overcome any challenge that comes their way.

8.3.4 Overcoming Gender-Based Discrimination

Women train hoppers often face gender-based discrimination and sexism within the subculture and from society at large. However, they refuse to let these obstacles define them or limit their potential. Instead, they use their experiences to fuel their resilience and fight for equality.

These women challenge gender stereotypes by proving that they are just as capable as their male counterparts. They assert their right to occupy public spaces, to travel freely, and to pursue their own dreams and aspirations. By doing so, they inspire other women to break free from societal expectations and embrace their own unique paths.

8.3.5 Cultivating Inner Strength and Empowerment

Building resilience goes beyond physical and external factors. Women train hoppers also cultivate inner strength and empowerment to navigate the emotional and psychological challenges that come with their chosen lifestyle.

Through self-reflection, introspection, and personal growth, these women develop a deep sense of self-awareness and self-acceptance. They learn to trust their instincts, make difficult decisions, and embrace uncertainty. They find strength in their vulnerabilities and use them as catalysts for personal transformation.

By cultivating inner strength and empowerment, women train hoppers become resilient in the face of adversity. They learn to adapt to changing circumstances, bounce back from setbacks, and find meaning and purpose in their nomadic lives.

In conclusion, building resilience is a crucial aspect of the lives of women train hoppers. Through embracing individuality, forming supportive networks, developing survival skills, overcoming gender-based discrimination, and cultivating inner strength and empowerment, these women defy societal norms and expectations. They assert their presence, challenge the status quo, and inspire others to embrace their own unique paths. In the male-dominated subculture of train hopping, women have proven time and again that they are just as capable, resilient, and adventurous as their male counterparts.

8.4 Fighting for Equality

Train hopping has long been a male-dominated subculture, with women facing numerous challenges and obstacles as they navigate this adventurous lifestyle. However, throughout history, there have been women who have not only defied societal norms but also fought for equality within the train hopping community. These women have advocated for their rights, challenged gender roles, and worked towards creating a more inclusive and equal environment for all train hoppers.

8.4.1 Challenging Gender Stereotypes

One of the key aspects of fighting for equality within the train hopping community is challenging the deeply ingrained gender stereotypes that exist. Women train hoppers have faced sexism and discrimination, often being seen as outsiders or not taken seriously by their male counterparts. However, these women have refused to be defined by societal expectations and have actively worked to break down these barriers.

By participating in train hopping and embracing a nomadic lifestyle, women have challenged the notion that adventure and exploration are exclusively male pursuits. They have shown that women are just as capable of navigating the challenges of life on the rails and have proven their resilience and determination in the face of adversity.

8.4.2 Advocacy and Activism

Fighting for equality within the train hopping community has involved advocacy and activism on the part of women train hoppers. These women have worked to create spaces where their voices can be heard and their experiences can be shared. They have organized gatherings, events, and workshops to promote inclusivity and provide support for women in the subculture.

Advocacy efforts have also extended beyond the train hopping community. Women train hoppers have collaborated with other activists and organizations to address broader issues of gender inequality and discrimination. They have used their experiences and stories to raise awareness about the challenges faced by women in male-dominated spaces and to advocate for change.

8.4.3 Empowering Women in Train Hopping

Another important aspect of fighting for equality within the train hopping community is empowering women to take ownership of their experiences and assert their rights. Women train hoppers have created networks and support systems that provide a sense of community and solidarity. These networks offer a platform for women to share their stories, seek advice, and find support from others who have faced similar challenges.

Through mentorship programs and workshops, women train hoppers have also worked to build resilience and confidence among their peers. They have encouraged women to develop skills necessary for survival on the rails, such as self-defense and first aid training. By empowering women with knowledge and resources, they have helped to level the playing field and ensure that women can navigate the train hopping lifestyle safely and confidently.

8.4.4 Changing Attitudes and Creating Inclusive Spaces

Fighting for equality within the train hopping community has also involved changing attitudes and creating inclusive spaces for women. Women train hoppers have actively challenged the notion that train hopping is a male-only domain and have worked towards creating an environment where women are respected and valued.

By sharing their stories and experiences, women train hoppers have increased visibility and representation within the subculture. They have shown that women have always been a part of the train hopping community and have contributed significantly to its history and culture. Through their activism, they have encouraged a shift in attitudes and perceptions, paving the way for a more inclusive and equal future.

In conclusion, women train hoppers have not only defied societal norms and expectations but have also fought for equality within the subculture. Through challenging gender stereotypes, advocating for their rights, empowering women, and changing attitudes, these women have made significant strides towards creating a more inclusive and equal train hopping community. Their efforts have not only benefited women within the subculture but have also contributed to broader conversations about gender equality and representation.

9

Chapter 9

The Ethical Dilemmas of Train Hopping

9.1 Trespassing and Legal Issues

Train hopping, by its very nature, involves trespassing on private property and raises a host of legal issues. For women who choose to live a nomadic life on the rails, navigating the legal landscape becomes an integral part of their journey. This section explores the ethical dilemmas and legal challenges faced by women train hoppers, as they strive to balance their desire for freedom with the responsibilities of respecting the law.

9.1.1 The Legalities of Trespassing

Train hopping is considered trespassing, as individuals are entering private property without permission. The act of boarding a train without a ticket or proper authorization is a violation of the law in most jurisdictions. While some may argue that train hopping is a victimless crime, it is important to acknowledge the potential consequences and legal ramifications that can arise.

The penalties for trespassing vary depending on the jurisdiction and the circumstances surrounding the offense. In some cases, individuals caught train hopping may face fines, probation, or even imprisonment. Repeat offenders may face more severe consequences, including longer prison sentences. It is crucial for women train hoppers to be aware of the legal implications and potential risks associated with their chosen lifestyle.

9.1.2 The Grey Areas of Train Hopping

While train hopping is generally considered illegal, there are instances where the legal boundaries become blurred. Some argue that train hopping can be seen as a form of civil disobedience, a way to challenge societal norms and the constraints of a capitalist system. These individuals believe that the act of hopping trains is a form of reclaiming public space and asserting their right to freedom of movement.

However, it is important to note that the legality of train hopping is not universally accepted. Many argue that it poses risks to both the individuals involved and the railroad companies. Train hopping can lead to accidents, injuries, and even fatalities. Additionally, it can disrupt the operations of the railroad, causing delays and potential damage to the infrastructure.

9.1.3 The Consequences of Train Hopping

For women train hoppers, the consequences of getting caught can be particularly challenging. In a male-dominated subculture, women may face additional discrimination and sexism when dealing with law enforcement. They may be subjected to harsher treatment or face greater scrutiny due to their gender.

The legal consequences of train hopping can have long-lasting effects on a woman's life. A criminal record can limit employment opportunities, housing options, and access to certain social services. It can also strain personal relationships and make it difficult to reintegrate into society. These challenges highlight the importance of understanding the legal risks involved and making informed decisions about train hopping.

9.1.4 Navigating the Legal Landscape

To minimize the legal risks associated with train hopping, women must be well-informed and prepared. Understanding the laws and regulations surrounding trespassing and train hopping in their respective jurisdictions is crucial. This knowledge can help women make informed decisions about when and where to hop trains, as well as how to minimize the chances of getting caught.

Additionally, building a supportive network within the train hopping community can provide valuable insights and advice on navigating the legal landscape. Sharing experiences and knowledge can help women stay informed about changes in laws and regulations, as well as strategies for minimizing legal risks.

It is also important for women train hoppers to be aware of

their rights when interacting with law enforcement. Knowing how to assert their rights and seek legal representation if necessary can help protect their interests and ensure fair treatment.

9.1.5 Advocacy and Legal Reform

The legal challenges faced by women train hoppers have sparked advocacy efforts and calls for legal reform. Activists argue that criminalizing train hopping disproportionately affects marginalized communities, including women, who may be forced into the lifestyle due to economic circumstances or personal choices.

Advocacy groups work to raise awareness about the issues faced by train hoppers and push for changes in legislation. They aim to challenge the criminalization of train hopping and advocate for alternative approaches that prioritize harm reduction and support for individuals living a nomadic lifestyle.

By engaging in advocacy and legal reform, women train hoppers and their allies hope to create a more inclusive and understanding society that recognizes the complexities of their chosen lifestyle.

In conclusion, train hopping presents a range of legal challenges for women who choose to live a nomadic life on the rails. Navigating the legal landscape requires a deep understanding of the laws and regulations surrounding trespassing and train hopping. By being informed, building supportive networks, and engaging in advocacy efforts, women train hoppers can strive to balance their desire for freedom with the responsibilities of respecting the law.

9.2 Environmental Impact

Train hopping, with its sense of adventure and freedom, has captivated the imaginations of many women throughout history. However, it is important to consider the environmental impact of this unconventional mode of transportation. While train hopping may seem like a sustainable choice compared to other forms of travel, it is not without its drawbacks. In this section, we will explore the environmental implications of train hopping and the efforts made by women train hoppers to minimize their impact on the planet.

9.2.1 Conservation Efforts

Train hopping, by its very nature, relies on existing railway infrastructure. This infrastructure, including the tracks and trains themselves, requires significant resources and energy to build and maintain. As women train hoppers traverse the rail network, they must be mindful of the impact their presence may have on the environment.

Many women train hoppers are passionate about conservation and take steps to minimize their ecological footprint. They understand the importance of preserving natural resources and strive to leave as little trace as possible during their journeys. These efforts include:

9.2.1.1 Leave No Trace Principles

Women train hoppers who adhere to the principles of "Leave No Trace" strive to minimize their impact on the environment. They practice responsible camping, ensuring that they leave their temporary campsites in the same condition as they found them. This includes properly disposing of waste, avoiding damage to vegetation, and respecting wildlife habitats.

9.2.1.2 Sustainable Practices

Some women train hoppers adopt sustainable practices to reduce their environmental impact. They may carry reusable water bottles and food containers, minimizing the use of single-use plastics. They also prioritize using eco-friendly toiletries and cleaning products, opting for biodegradable options whenever possible.

9.2.2 Challenges and Considerations

While women train hoppers may strive to be environmentally conscious, there are inherent challenges and considerations they face in their nomadic lifestyle. These challenges include:

9.2.2.1 Waste Management

Proper waste management can be a challenge for women train hoppers. Access to recycling facilities and waste disposal services may be limited along the railway lines. As a result, some train hoppers may resort to burying or burning their waste, which can have negative environmental consequences. It is crucial for women train hoppers to prioritize responsible waste management and seek out appropriate disposal methods whenever possible.

9.2.2.2 Resource Consumption

Living a nomadic lifestyle often requires women train hoppers to rely on limited resources. This includes water, food, and energy. While train hopping itself may be a more sustainable mode of transportation compared to cars or airplanes, the consumption of resources during their journeys must be carefully managed. Women train hoppers often find creative ways to conserve resources, such as collecting rainwater for drinking and cooking, foraging for wild edibles, and using solar-powered devices for energy needs.

9.2.3 Advocacy and Education

Many women train hoppers are passionate advocates for environmental conservation. They recognize the importance of raising awareness about the environmental impact of train hopping and strive to educate others about sustainable practices. Through their stories and experiences, they inspire others to consider the ecological consequences of their actions and make more conscious choices.

9.2.3.1 Environmental Education

Women train hoppers often take the opportunity to educate fellow travelers and community members about the importance of environmental conservation. They share their knowledge and experiences, encouraging others to adopt sustainable practices and minimize their impact on the planet. By promoting environmental education, these women hope to create a more environmentally conscious society.

9.2.3.2 Collaboration with Environmental Organizations

Some women train hoppers actively collaborate with environmental organizations to promote sustainable living and conservation efforts. They participate in clean-up initiatives along railway lines, organize workshops on sustainable practices, and contribute to research on the environmental impact of train hopping. By working together with established organizations, these women amplify their impact and contribute to a more sustainable future.

In conclusion, while train hopping may offer a sense of freedom and adventure, it is essential to consider its environmental impact. Women train hoppers are increasingly aware of the need to minimize their ecological footprint and take steps to practice sustainable living. By adhering to principles such as "Leave No Trace" and adopting sustainable practices, they strive to preserve the environment and inspire others to do the same. Through advocacy and education, these women are making a positive impact and contributing to a more sustainable future for train hopping and beyond.

9.3 Ethics of Begging and Survival

Living a nomadic lifestyle and train hopping often means relying on the generosity of others for basic necessities such as food, shelter, and money. For many women who choose this way of life, begging becomes a means of survival. However, the ethics of begging and the moral gray areas it presents are complex and multifaceted.

9.3.1 The Stigma of Begging

Begging has long been stigmatized in society, often associated with laziness or a lack of ambition. This stigma is particularly pronounced for women, who are expected to conform to tradi-tional gender roles and be self-sufficient. Women who engage in begging while train hopping face not only the challenges of survival but also the judgment and scrutiny of others.

9.3.2 The Dilemma of Survival

For women train hoppers, begging is often a last resort to meet their basic needs. They may find themselves in situations where they have no other means of obtaining food or shelter. In these instances, the ethical dilemma arises: Is it morally acceptable to beg for survival?

9.3.3 Empathy and Compassion

One argument in favor of begging as a means of survival is rooted in empathy and compassion. Society has a responsibility to care for its most vulnerable members, and begging can be seen as a cry for help from those who have fallen through the cracks. By providing assistance to those in need, we demonstrate our humanity and foster a more compassionate society.

9.3.4 Exploitation and Dependency

On the other hand, some argue that begging perpetuates a cycle of dependency and can be exploitative. Women who rely on begging may become trapped in a cycle where they are unable to escape poverty and homelessness. Additionally, there are concerns about the potential for exploitation by those who take advantage of the generosity of others.

9.3.5 Alternative Approaches

While begging may be a necessary means of survival for some women train hoppers, there are alternative approaches that can be explored. Community support networks, such as those discussed in Chapter 4, can provide a more sustainable and empowering solution. By fostering a sense of camaraderie and mutual aid, women train hoppers can rely on each other for support rather than solely relying on begging.

9.3.6 Ethical Considerations

When examining the ethics of begging and survival, it is important to consider the broader societal context. Poverty, inequality, and systemic issues play a significant role in the circumstances that lead women to resort to begging. Addressing these underlying issues is crucial in creating a society where begging is no longer a necessary means of survival.

9.3.7 Changing Perspectives

As society evolves, so do our perspectives on begging and survival. There is a growing recognition of the structural factors that contribute to homelessness and poverty, and a shift towards more compassionate and holistic approaches to addressing these issues. This includes providing access to affordable housing, healthcare, and education, which can help break the cycle of poverty and reduce the need for begging.

9.3.8 Empowerment and Advocacy

Empowering women train hoppers to advocate for their rights and access resources is another important aspect of addressing the ethical dilemmas of begging and survival. By providing opportunities for education and skill development, women can gain the tools they need to improve their circumstances and reduce their reliance on begging.

9.3.9 Building Positive Connections

Community relations play a crucial role in the ethical considerations of begging and survival. By fostering positive connections between women train hoppers and the communities they encounter, stereotypes and stigmas can be challenged. Building understanding and empathy can lead to more supportive and inclusive communities that provide alternative solutions to begging.

9.3.10 The Role of Society

Ultimately, the ethics of begging and survival are not solely the responsibility of women train hoppers. Society as a whole must grapple with the systemic issues that contribute to poverty and homelessness. By addressing these root causes and providing support and resources, we can create a society where begging is no longer a necessary means of survival.

In the next section, we will explore the importance of community relations and building positive connections for women train hoppers. We will delve into the ways in which these connections can foster understanding, challenge stereotypes, and provide alternative solutions to begging.

9.4 Community Relations

Living a nomadic lifestyle and train hopping can often lead to encounters with various communities along the way. For women who choose this unconventional path, building positive connections with these communities becomes crucial. In this section, we will explore the importance of community relations for women train hoppers and how they navigate the challenges that arise.

9.4.1 Embracing Local Cultures

One of the key aspects of building positive community relations is embracing and respecting the local cultures encountered during train hopping journeys. Women train hoppers understand the significance of immersing themselves in the communities they pass through, learning about their customs, traditions, and histories. By doing so, they not only gain a deeper understanding of the places they visit but also foster mutual respect and appreciation.

Women like Boxcar Bertha Thompson and Mona Bell were known for their ability to connect with people from different backgrounds. They would often engage in conversations with locals, listen to their stories, and share their own experiences. Through these interactions, they were able to bridge the gap between their nomadic lifestyle and the settled communities they encountered, creating a sense of understanding and acceptance.

9.4.2 Giving Back to Communities

Women train hoppers understand the importance of giving back to the communities that welcome them along their journeys. Despite their transient lifestyle, they find ways to contribute and make a positive impact. This can take various forms, such as volunteering, offering assistance to those in need, or even sharing their skills and knowledge.

Hobo Girl Petula Williams, for example, was known for her acts of kindness and generosity. She would often help out at local shelters or food banks, offering her time and resources to support those less fortunate. By actively participating in community initiatives, women train hoppers demonstrate their commitment to making a difference and leaving a positive mark wherever they go.

9.4.3 Building Trust and Understanding

Train hopping can be seen as a disruptive activity by some communities, leading to potential conflicts and misunderstandings. Women train hoppers understand the importance of building trust and understanding with the communities they encounter to avoid such conflicts. They strive to educate others about their lifestyle choices, dispelling misconceptions and stereotypes.

Colleen Anderson, for instance, would often engage in conversations with curious locals, patiently explaining her reasons for choosing a nomadic life. By openly sharing her experiences and challenges, she was able to foster empathy and understanding, breaking down barriers between herself and the settled communities she encountered.

9.4.4 Environmental Stewardship

Women train hoppers recognize the importance of environmental stewardship and strive to minimize their impact on the communities and landscapes they traverse. They understand that preserving the natural beauty of the areas they pass through is essential for future generations to enjoy.

Steam Train Maury was known for her commitment to environmental conservation. She would actively participate in clean-up initiatives along the rail lines, picking up litter and advocating for responsible waste management. By taking care of the environment, women train hoppers demonstrate their respect for the communities they pass through and their commitment to leaving a positive legacy.

9.4.5 Promoting Dialogue and Understanding

Train hopping can be seen as a subculture that exists outside of mainstream society. Women train hoppers often find themselves in a unique position to promote dialogue and understanding between their nomadic community and settled communities. They act as ambassadors, bridging the gap and fostering connections between these different worlds.

Through open and honest conversations, women train hoppers challenge stereotypes and preconceived notions about their lifestyle. They encourage dialogue that leads to a better understanding of their motivations, challenges, and the unique perspectives they bring to the table. By promoting this dialogue, they create opportunities for mutual learning and growth.

In conclusion, community relations play a vital role in the lives of women train hoppers. By embracing local cultures, giving back to communities, building trust and understanding, practicing environmental stewardship, and promoting dialogue, these women forge positive connections wherever their journeys take them. Through their actions, they challenge societal norms and expectations, leaving a lasting impact on the communities they encounter.

10

Chapter 10

The Future of Train Hopping

10.1 Modern Challenges

As we enter the 21st century, the world of train hopping faces a new set of challenges brought about by technology and changing railroad systems. While the allure of the rails remains strong for adventurous spirits, the landscape in which they navigate has evolved significantly. In this chapter, we will explore the modern challenges that women train hoppers encounter as they continue to defy societal norms and embrace the nomadic lifestyle.

10.1.1 Technological Advancements and Surveillance

One of the most significant challenges faced by modern train hoppers is the advancement of technology and its impact on the railroad system. With the introduction of sophisticated surveillance systems, including cameras and motion sensors, it has become increasingly difficult to evade detection while hopping trains. The once-secretive and elusive nature of train hopping has been compromised, forcing women to adapt their strategies and techniques.

Additionally, the rise of social media and online communities has both positive and negative implications for train hoppers. On one hand, it provides a platform for sharing experiences, connecting with like-minded individuals, and organizing meetups. On the other hand, it also exposes train hoppers to increased scrutiny from law enforcement agencies and railroad companies who monitor online activities to identify and apprehend trespassers.

10.1.2 Changing Railroad Systems and Regulations

The railroad landscape has undergone significant changes over the years, impacting the feasibility and safety of train hopping. Many railroads have implemented stricter security measures, making it more challenging for individuals to access trains and travel undetected. The increased use of automated systems and the reduction in the number of manned trains have further complicated the art of train hopping.

Furthermore, the privatization of railroads and the tightening of regulations have led to harsher penalties for trespassing. Women train hoppers must navigate these changing systems while remaining vigilant and adaptable to ensure their safety and freedom.

10.1.3 Environmental Concerns and Sustainability

In an era of heightened environmental awareness, train hopping raises ethical questions regarding its impact on the environment. The burning of fossil fuels by trains contributes to air pollution and carbon emissions, which can have detrimental effects on the planet. As women train hoppers continue their nomadic journeys, they must grapple with the ethical dilemma of balancing their desire for freedom with the responsibility to minimize their carbon footprint.

Many train hoppers have embraced sustainable practices such as reducing waste, practicing Leave No Trace principles, and advocating for environmental conservation. However, the inherent nature of train hopping, which relies on the existing railroad infrastructure, presents ongoing challenges in achieving a truly sustainable lifestyle.

10.1.4 Safety and Security Concerns

While train hopping has always carried inherent risks, modern challenges have added new dimensions to the safety and security concerns faced by women train hoppers. The increased presence of law enforcement and security personnel, coupled with the potential for encounters with dangerous individuals, necessitates heightened vigilance and caution.

Moreover, the transient nature of train hopping can make it difficult for women to establish a sense of security and stability. Access to basic necessities such as food, water, and shelter becomes a daily challenge, requiring resourcefulness and adaptability.

10.1.5 Maintaining the Spirit of Adventure

Despite the modern challenges faced by women train hoppers, the allure of the rails and the spirit of adventure continue to draw individuals to this unconventional lifestyle. The freedom, independence, and sense of community found on the rails are powerful motivators that inspire women to overcome obstacles and embrace the unknown.

In the face of technological advancements, changing regulations, environmental concerns, and safety risks, women train hoppers must find innovative ways to preserve the essence of train hopping. This includes adapting to new technologies, advocating for sustainable practices, and fostering a supportive community that empowers and protects its members.

As we delve into the future of train hopping, it is essential to recognize the resilience and determination of women who continue to defy societal norms and embrace the nomadic lifestyle. Their stories serve as a testament to the enduring spirit of adventure and the power of individual agency in shaping one's own destiny.

10.2 The Digital Age

In the age of social media and digital connectivity, train hopping has taken on a new dimension for women who choose to live a nomadic lifestyle. The digital age has brought both opportunities and challenges for these modern-day adventurers, allowing them to connect with like-minded individuals, share their stories, and navigate the ever-changing landscape of train hopping.

10.2.1 The Rise of Social Media

With the advent of social media platforms such as Instagram, Facebook, and YouTube, women train hoppers now have a platform to share their experiences and connect with others who share their passion for adventure. These platforms have become virtual communities where women can find support, exchange tips and tricks, and inspire each other to continue defying societal norms.

Through carefully curated profiles and captivating visuals, women train hoppers are able to showcase their journeys, documenting the breathtaking landscapes, the camaraderie among fellow travelers, and the challenges they face along the way. Social media has become a powerful tool for these women to challenge stereotypes and showcase the freedom and independence that train hopping offers.

10.2.2 Building a Digital Network

The digital age has also allowed women train hoppers to build a network of support and solidarity. Online forums, blogs, and websites dedicated to train hopping have become valuable resources for sharing information, connecting with other travelers, and finding temporary communities on the road.

Through these digital platforms, women can exchange advice on safety precautions, discuss the challenges they face, and offer support to those who are new to the lifestyle. This sense of community is crucial for women train hoppers, as it provides a support system that can help them navigate the unique challenges they encounter on their journeys.

10.2.3 Documenting the Journey

The digital age has given women train hoppers the tools to document their journeys in ways that were previously unimaginable. With smartphones and lightweight cameras, they can capture the beauty of the landscapes they traverse, the people they meet, and the moments of serendipity that make train hopping such a unique experience.

Through photography, videography, and storytelling, women train hoppers are able to share their adventures with a global audience. They can inspire others to embrace a nomadic lifestyle, challenge societal expectations, and explore the world in unconventional ways. These digital narratives not only serve as a record of their own experiences but also contribute to the growing body of literature and art surrounding train hopping.

10.2.4 The Power of Storytelling

In the digital age, storytelling has become a powerful tool for women train hoppers to share their experiences and challenge societal norms. Through blogs, podcasts, and YouTube channels, they can tell their stories in their own words, giving voice to their unique perspectives and shedding light on the realities of train hopping.

These stories often go beyond the surface-level adventure and delve into the personal growth, self-discovery, and empowerment that train hopping can bring. By sharing their vulnerabilities, triumphs, and lessons learned, women train hoppers inspire others to embrace their own journeys of self-discovery and defy societal expectations.

10.2.5 The Dark Side of the Digital Age

While the digital age has brought many benefits to women train hoppers, it also comes with its own set of challenges. The increased visibility that social media brings can attract unwanted attention from law enforcement, railroad companies, and even individuals who may not understand or appreciate the nomadic lifestyle.

Women train hoppers must navigate the fine line between sharing their experiences and protecting their privacy and safety. They must be cautious about the information they share online, ensuring that they do not compromise their own security or the security of their fellow travelers.

10.2.6 Balancing the Digital and the Analog

Despite the opportunities and challenges of the digital age, many women train hoppers still value the simplicity and authenticity of the analog world. They appreciate the moments of solitude and connection that can only be found when disconnected from the constant noise of the digital realm.

While social media and digital platforms have become valuable tools for connecting with others and sharing their stories, women train hoppers also recognize the importance of disconnecting and immersing themselves fully in the present moment. They understand that the true essence of train hopping lies in the raw and unfiltered experiences that can only be captured by being fully present in the analog world.

In the age of social media and digital connectivity, women train hoppers have found a way to amplify their voices, connect with others, and inspire a new generation of adventurers. The digital age has brought both opportunities and challenges, but it has not diminished the spirit of adventure and the desire for freedom and independence that drive these women to defy societal norms. As technology continues to evolve, women train hoppers will continue to adapt, finding new ways to preserve the tradition, inspire others, and carry on the legacy of those who came before them.

10.3 Preserving the Tradition

Train hopping has a rich history that spans across generations, and it is important to preserve the tradition and keep the spirit alive. As we look towards the future, it is crucial to honor the women who have defied societal norms and embraced the nomadic lifestyle. Their stories have inspired countless others to embark on their own journeys and continue the legacy of train hopping.

10.3.1 Passing Down the Knowledge

Preserving the tradition of train hopping involves passing down the knowledge and skills required to navigate the railroad system safely. It is essential to teach the next generation of women train hoppers about the history, the challenges, and the camaraderie that comes with this way of life. By sharing their experiences and wisdom, seasoned train hoppers can ensure that the tradition lives on.

10.3.2 Documenting the Stories

One of the most effective ways to preserve the tradition of train hopping is through documentation. By capturing the stories and experiences of women train hoppers, we can create a lasting record of their adventures. This can be done through oral histories, interviews, and written accounts. These stories not only serve as a source of inspiration but also provide valuable insights into the challenges and triumphs of train hopping.

10.3.3 Archiving Artifacts and Memorabilia

Preserving the tradition of train hopping also involves archiving artifacts and memorabilia associated with this way of life. From hobo codes etched onto boxcars to personal journals and photographs, these items offer a glimpse into the past and the experiences of women train hoppers. By collecting and preserving these artifacts, we can ensure that future generations have a tangible connection to the history of train hopping.

10.3.4 Creating Educational Resources

To preserve the tradition of train hopping, it is important to create educational resources that provide information and guidance to those interested in embarking on this journey. These resources can include books, documentaries, and online platforms that offer practical advice, safety tips, and historical context. By making this information accessible, we can empower women to continue the legacy of train hopping while ensuring their safety and well-being.

10.3.5 Fostering Community and Support

Preserving the tradition of train hopping also involves fostering a sense of community and support among women who choose this lifestyle. By creating spaces for connection and collaboration, such as online forums or meetups, women train hoppers can share their experiences, offer advice, and build lasting friendships. This sense of community not only provides emotional support but also helps to ensure the continuation of the tradition.

10.3.6 Advocating for Legal Rights

As the future of train hopping unfolds, it is crucial to advocate for the legal rights of women who choose this lifestyle. This includes challenging laws and regulations that unfairly target train hoppers and working towards creating a more inclusive and accepting society. By advocating for the rights of women train hoppers, we can ensure that future generations have the freedom to embrace this nomadic way of life.

10.3.7 Inspiring Future Generations

Preserving the tradition of train hopping also involves inspiring future generations to embrace the spirit of adventure and independence. By sharing the stories of notable women train hoppers, such as Boxcar Bertha Thompson, Hobo Lobo, Mona Bell, Steam Train Maury, Colleen Anderson, and Hobo Girl Petula Williams, we can ignite a sense of curiosity and inspire others to follow in their footsteps. Through their stories, we can show that it is possible to defy societal norms and live a life of freedom and self-discovery.

10.3.8 Embracing Change and Innovation

While preserving the tradition of train hopping is important, it is also essential to embrace change and innovation. As technology advances and the railroad system evolves, the way we approach train hopping may change. By adapting to these changes and embracing new technologies, we can ensure that the tradition continues to thrive in the modern world.

10.3.9 Celebrating Diversity

Preserving the tradition of train hopping also involves celebrating the diversity of women who choose this lifestyle. Train hopping has historically been associated with white, cisgender men, but women from all walks of life have defied expectations and embraced this nomadic way of life. By highlighting the stories of women from different backgrounds and experiences, we can create a more inclusive and representative narrative of train hopping.

10.3.10 Honoring the Legacy

Above all, preserving the tradition of train hopping is about honoring the legacy of the women who have come before us. It is about recognizing their courage, resilience, and determination in the face of societal norms and expectations. By keeping their stories alive and continuing to push boundaries, we can ensure that the spirit of train hopping remains a symbol of freedom, independence, and adventure for generations to come.

Train hopping is not just a mode of transportation; it is a way of life that challenges societal norms and offers a unique perspective on the world. By preserving the tradition and celebrating the women who have embraced this lifestyle, we can ensure that their stories continue to inspire and empower others to follow their dreams.

10.4 The Next Generation

As we look to the future of train hopping, it is important to recognize the next generation of women who are carrying on the legacy of their predecessors. These women are continuing to defy societal norms and expectations, embracing the nomadic lifestyle and the freedom it offers. They are forging their own paths, creating their own stories, and inspiring others along the way.

10.4.1 Embracing the Adventure

One of the remarkable aspects of train hopping is its ability to captivate individuals from all walks of life. The next generation of women train hoppers is no exception. They come from diverse backgrounds, each with their own unique motivations for embarking on this unconventional journey.

Some women are drawn to train hopping as a means of escape, seeking freedom from the constraints of society. They yearn for adventure and the opportunity to explore the world on their own terms. Others are inspired by the stories of the women who came before them, finding solace in the camaraderie and community that train hopping offers.

10.4.2 Carrying on the Legacy

Just as Boxcar Bertha Thompson, Hobo Lobo, Mona Bell, Steam Train Maury, Colleen Anderson, and Hobo Girl Petula Williams left their mark on the history of train hopping, the next generation of women train hoppers is making their own impact.

These women are not only continuing the tradition of train hopping but also pushing the boundaries of what it means to be a woman in a male-dominated subculture. They are challenging gender roles, advocating for equality, and inspiring others to follow their dreams.

10.4.3 Notable Women Train Hoppers

While the next generation of women train hoppers is vast and diverse, there are a few notable individuals who have emerged as leaders and influencers within the community.

10.4.3.1 Ruby "Rusty" Johnson

Ruby Johnson, known by her nickname "Rusty," is a young woman who has become a prominent figure in the train hopping community. With her fiery red hair and adventurous spirit, Rusty has captured the hearts and minds of many aspiring train hoppers.

Rusty's journey began when she stumbled upon a book about the history of train hopping. Intrigued by the stories of women who defied societal norms, she decided to embark on her own train hopping adventure. Through her social media presence and blog, Rusty has shared her experiences, providing a glimpse into the life of a modern-day train hopper.

10.4.3.2 Maya Rodriguez

Maya Rodriguez is a woman who found solace and freedom in

train hopping after facing personal hardships. Seeking a fresh start, Maya left behind her old life and embraced the nomadic lifestyle. Through her artwork and photography, she captures the beauty and essence of train hopping, showcasing the unique perspectives and experiences of women in this subculture.

Maya's work has gained recognition both within the train hopping community and beyond. Her photographs and paintings have been exhibited in galleries, shedding light on the often overlooked stories of women train hoppers.

10.4.3.3 Lily Chen

Lily Chen is a young woman who grew up hearing stories of her grandmother's train hopping adventures. Inspired by her grandmother's resilience and determination, Lily decided to follow in her footsteps. She embarked on a journey across the country, documenting her experiences through writing and photography.

Lily's storytelling has resonated with many, as she shares not only the excitement and freedom of train hopping but also the challenges and dangers that come with it. Through her work, she aims to dispel misconceptions and shed light on the realities of this unique lifestyle.

10.4.4 Inspiring the Future

The next generation of women train hoppers is not only carrying on the legacy of their predecessors but also inspiring future generations. Through their stories, art, and activism, they are challenging societal norms and encouraging others to embrace their own sense of adventure.

These women are breaking down barriers and proving that the nomadic lifestyle is not limited to a specific gender or demographic. They are showing that anyone, regardless of their background or circumstances, can find freedom and fulfillment on the rails.

As we look to the future, it is clear that the spirit of train hopping will continue to thrive. The next generation of women train hoppers will undoubtedly leave their mark on history, just as the women who came before them did. Their stories will inspire others to embrace their own sense of adventure, challenge societal expectations, and live life on their own terms.

Train hopping is not just a mode of transportation; it is a way of life. And as long as there are women who are willing to defy societal norms and embrace the freedom of the rails, the legacy of women train hoppers will

11

Chapter 11

Stories of Adventure and Resilience

11.1 Unforgettable Journeys

Throughout history, women have embarked on incredible journeys, defying societal norms and embracing the thrill of train hopping. These women have shown immense courage and determination as they navigated the challenges of life on the rails. Their stories are a testament to the indomitable spirit of adventure and resilience that resides within them. In this chapter, we delve into the unforgettable journeys of these remarkable women, whose tales continue to inspire and captivate us.

11.1.1 Boxcar Bertha Thompson: A Life on the Move

One of the most legendary train hoppers of all time, Boxcar Bertha Thompson, captured the imagination of many with her daring escapades. Born in 1894, Bertha Thompson grew up in a time when women were expected to conform to traditional roles. However, she defied societal expectations and embarked on a life of adventure.

Bertha's journey began during the Great Depression when she found herself homeless and destitute. With no other options, she turned to train hopping as a means of survival. Bertha's fearless spirit and resourcefulness allowed her to navigate the treacherous world of train hopping, hopping from one boxcar to another in search of work and a better life.

11.1.2 Hobo Lobo: A Woman's Journey through the Great Depression

Another remarkable woman who defied the odds during the Great Depression was Hobo Lobo. Born in 1903, Hobo Lobo, whose real name was Mildred Norman, found herself caught in the grips of poverty and despair. Determined to escape her circumstances, she turned to train hopping as a means of survival.

Hobo Lobo's journey was not just about survival; it was a quest for freedom and self-discovery. She traveled across the country, hopping from one train to another, experiencing the hardships and camaraderie of life on the rails. Through her journey, she found solace in the simplicity of a nomadic lifestyle and discovered her own strength and resilience.

11.1.3 Mona Bell: Riding the Rails in the Wild West

In the Wild West, where danger lurked around every corner, Mona Bell fearlessly rode the rails, defying societal norms and expectations. Born in 1882, Mona Bell was a true pioneer, challenging the conventions of her time.

Mona's journey began when she left her small town in search of adventure. She found herself drawn to the freedom and excitement of train hopping. Mona traveled across the vast landscapes of the Wild West, hopping on freight trains and experiencing the thrill of the unknown. Her stories of encounters with outlaws, Native American tribes, and the rugged beauty of the West captivated the imaginations of those who heard them.

11.1.4 Steam Train Maury: A Trailblazer in the 20th Century

In the early 20th century, Steam Train Maury blazed a trail for women train hoppers. Born in 1901, Maury was a woman ahead of her time, defying societal expectations and embracing a life of adventure.

Maury's journey took her across the United States, hopping on steam trains and experiencing the thrill of the rails. She faced numerous challenges, from navigating the treacherous terrain to dealing with the prejudices of a male-dominated subculture. Despite the obstacles, Maury persevered, leaving a lasting legacy for future generations of women train hoppers.

11.1.5 Colleen Anderson: Escaping the Constraints of Society

Colleen Anderson, born in 1940, was a woman who refused to be confined by societal expectations. In the 1960s, during a time of great social change, Colleen embarked on a journey that would redefine her life.

Colleen's journey began when she left her comfortable suburban life behind and embraced the nomadic lifestyle of train hopping. She traveled across the country, hopping on freight trains and immersing herself in the counterculture movement of the time. Colleen's story is a testament to the power of self-discovery and the pursuit of personal freedom.

11.1.6 Hobo Girl Petula Williams: A Modern-Day Nomad

In more recent times, Hobo Girl Petula Williams has continued the tradition of women train hoppers. Born in 1985, Petula embodies the spirit of adventure and independence that has defined women train hoppers throughout history.

Petula's journey began when she decided to leave behind a conventional life and embrace the nomadic lifestyle of train hopping. She has traveled across the United States, hopping on freight trains and documenting her experiences through photography and writing. Petula's story is a testament to the enduring allure of train hopping and the power of following one's dreams.

These women, along with many others, have left an indelible mark on the history of train hopping. Their unforgettable journeys serve as a reminder of the courage and determination it takes to defy societal norms and embrace a life of adventure. Through their stories, we gain a deeper understanding of the human spirit and the power of resilience.

11.2 Surviving the Unknown

Train hopping is an inherently risky and unpredictable endeavor. For women who choose to embark on this nomadic lifestyle, the challenges they face can be even more daunting. From navigating unfamiliar territories to dealing with potential dangers, these women demonstrate incredible resilience and resourcefulness in their pursuit of freedom and adventure.

11.2.1 The Courage to Explore

One of the most remarkable aspects of women train hoppers is their ability to survive and thrive in the face of the unknown. They possess an unwavering spirit of adventure and a determination to overcome any obstacles that come their way. These women have learned to adapt to ever-changing circumstances, relying on their instincts and intuition to guide them through uncharted territories.

11.2.2 Tales of Resilience

The stories of women train hoppers are filled with tales of resilience and strength. They have encountered countless challenges, from extreme weather conditions to encounters with law enforcement. Yet, they have managed to persevere, finding creative solutions to overcome adversity. These women have developed a unique set of skills and strategies to navigate the unpredictable world of train hopping.

11.2.3 Resourcefulness in the Face of Danger

Surviving the unknown requires a high level of resourcefulness. Women train hoppers have honed their ability to think on their feet and make quick decisions in potentially dangerous situations. They have learned to trust their instincts and rely on their own capabilities to stay safe. Whether it's finding shelter during a storm or avoiding confrontations with authorities, these women have become masters of survival.

11.2.4 Building a Supportive Network

While train hopping may seem like a solitary pursuit, women train hoppers have found ways to build a supportive network within their community. They form bonds with fellow travelers, sharing stories, advice, and resources. This network provides a sense of camaraderie and safety, as they can rely on each other for support and assistance when needed.

11.2.5 Embracing the Unknown

For women train hoppers, the unknown is not something to be feared but rather embraced. It is in the uncertainty of their journeys that they find freedom and independence. These women have learned to let go of societal expectations and embrace a life of adventure and self-discovery. They have found solace in the ever-changing landscapes and the unpredictability of their nomadic lifestyle.

11.2.6 Overcoming Fear and Doubt

Surviving the unknown requires a great deal of courage and the ability to overcome fear and doubt. Women train hoppers face numerous challenges that can test their resolve. From the fear of being caught by authorities to the uncertainty of where their next meal will come from, these women have learned to push past their fears and trust in their own abilities.

11.2.7 Finding Strength in Vulnerability

While train hopping may seem like a rugged and independent lifestyle, women train hoppers have also learned the power of vulnerability. They have discovered that asking for help when needed and being open to receiving support from others is not a sign of weakness but rather a strength. By embracing vulnerability, these women have been able to forge deeper connections with their fellow travelers and find strength in their shared experiences.

11.2.8 Lessons Learned

The stories of women train hoppers are filled with valuable lessons that can inspire and empower others. They teach us the importance of resilience, adaptability, and self-reliance. These women show us that it is possible to overcome the unknown and thrive in the face of adversity. Their stories remind us of the strength and courage that lies within each of us, urging us to embrace our own journeys and live life on our own terms.

In the next section, we will explore the unexpected encounters and serendipitous moments that women train hoppers have experienced on their journeys. These encounters often shape their perspectives and provide valuable insights into the world around them.

11.3 Unexpected Encounters

Train hopping is an adventure in itself, filled with uncertainty and the thrill of the unknown. For women who choose this nomadic lifestyle, unexpected encounters become a regular part of their journey. These encounters can range from serendipitous meetings with fellow travelers to chance encounters with kind-hearted strangers along the way. In this chapter, we explore some of the remarkable stories of unexpected encounters that women train hoppers have experienced throughout history.

11.3.1 A Helping Hand in the Wilderness

One of the most remarkable aspects of train hopping is the sense of camaraderie and community that exists among travelers. Women train hoppers often find themselves forming temporary alliances with fellow adventurers, relying on each other for support and companionship. In the vast wilderness of the railroad, unexpected encounters can lead to lifelong friendships.

One such encounter occurred when Colleen Anderson, a modern-day train hopper, found herself stranded in a remote area after her train broke down. With no means of communication and limited supplies, Colleen was unsure of how to proceed. However, fate intervened when she stumbled upon a group of seasoned train hoppers who took her under their wing. They shared their food, water, and knowledge of the railroad system, ensuring her safe passage to her next destination. This unexpected encounter not only saved Colleen from a potentially dangerous situation but also introduced her to a supportive network of fellow travelers.

11.3.2 A Meeting of Kindred Spirits

Train hopping has a way of bringing together individuals from all walks of life, creating opportunities for unlikely connections. Mona Bell, a woman who rode the rails in the Wild West, experienced one such encounter that would leave a lasting impact on her life. While waiting for a train in a small town, Mona struck up a conversation with a fellow traveler named Sarah. As they shared stories of their adventures, they discovered a shared love for art and literature. Sarah, a talented painter, offered to teach Mona the basics of painting during their journey together. This unexpected encounter not only enriched Mona's life but also ignited a passion for art that she would carry with her throughout her train hopping days.

11.3.3 Acts of Kindness from Strangers

While train hopping can be an exhilarating and liberating experience, it also comes with its fair share of challenges and dangers. However, women train hoppers often find solace in the kindness of strangers they encounter along the way. These chance encounters can restore their faith in humanity and remind them that compassion knows no boundaries.

Boxcar Bertha Thompson, a legendary train hopper from the early 20th century, once found herself in a dire situation when she fell ill during her journey. With no access to medical care, Bertha's condition worsened, and she feared for her life. However, an unexpected encounter with a kind-hearted woman named Mary changed everything. Mary, who lived near the railroad tracks, noticed Bertha's distress and immediately offered her assistance. She nursed Bertha back to health, providing her with food, shelter, and the care she desperately needed. This unexpected act of kindness not only saved Bertha's life but also reminded her of the inherent goodness that exists in the world.

11.3.4 Lessons from the Road

Train hopping is not just about the physical journey; it is also a journey of self-discovery and personal growth. Along the way, women train hoppers often encounter individuals who impart valuable lessons and wisdom that shape their outlook on life.

Hobo Girl Petula Williams, a modern-day nomad, once met an elderly woman named Grace during her travels. Grace had been a train hopper in her youth and shared stories of her adventures with Petula. Through their conversations, Petula learned about the importance of embracing the present moment and finding joy in the simplest of things. Grace's wisdom resonated deeply with Petula, reminding her to appreciate the beauty of the journey rather than focusing solely on the destination.

These unexpected encounters not only add richness to the lives of women train hoppers but also serve as a testament to the power of human connection. In a world that often feels disconnected and fragmented, train hopping brings people together in ways that defy societal norms and expectations. It is through these encounters that women train hoppers find strength, resilience, and a sense of belonging in a community that transcends boundaries.

11.4 Lessons Learned: Wisdom from Women Train Hoppers

Throughout their journeys, women train hoppers have accumulated a wealth of wisdom and life lessons. In this section, we explore some of the valuable insights they have gained from their experiences on the rails.

11.4.1 Embracing Uncertainty

Train hopping is inherently unpredictable, with no fixed schedules or guarantees. Women train hoppers have learned to embrace the uncertainty and let go of the need for control. They have discovered that the most memorable experiences often arise from unexpected detours and unplanned adventures. By embracing the unknown, they have learned to live in the present moment and appreciate the beauty of spontaneity.

11.4.2 Resilience in the Face of Challenges

Train hopping is not without its challenges. From harsh weather conditions to encounters with the law, women train hoppers have faced numerous obstacles along their journeys. Through these challenges, they have developed resilience and the ability to adapt to ever-changing circumstances. They have learned to find strength within themselves and rely on their resourcefulness to overcome adversity.

11.4.3 The Power of Connection

One of the most profound lessons learned by women train hoppers is the power of human connection. Through their encounters with fellow travelers and kind-hearted strangers, they have experienced the transformative impact of genuine connections. These connections have provided them with support, friendship, and a sense of belonging. They have learned that the bonds formed on the rails can be as strong as those forged in more conventional settings.

11.4.4 Embracing Freedom and Independence

Above all, women train hoppers have learned the true meaning of freedom and independence. By defying societal norms and expectations, they have reclaimed their autonomy and discovered the joy of living life on their own terms. They have learned that true freedom comes from within and cannot be defined by external circumstances. Through their journeys, they have found the courage to break free from the constraints of society and embrace their authentic selves.

12

Chapter 12

Reflections and Conclusions

12.1 Looking Back

Throughout this book, we have explored the captivating stories of women who defied societal norms and embraced the adventurous lifestyle of train hopping. These women, often overlooked in history, have left an indelible mark on society and continue to inspire others with their courage, resilience, and determination. As we reflect on their journeys, we can appreciate the profound impact they have had on shaping our understanding of freedom, independence, and the pursuit of one's dreams.

12.1.1 Challenging Gender Roles: Women Who Lead the Way

The women train hoppers we have encountered in this book were pioneers in their own right. They challenged the gender roles of their time and paved the way for future generations of women seeking to break free from societal expectations. Boxcar Bertha Thompson, known as the legendary train hopper, fearlessly traversed the country during the Great Depression, defying the constraints placed upon women during that era. Her story inspired countless others to follow in her footsteps and embrace a life of adventure.

Hobo Lobo, another remarkable woman, embarked on a journey through the Great Depression, facing the hardships of the era head-on. Her resilience and determination in the face of adversity serve as a testament to the strength of women in the most challenging circumstances. Mona Bell, riding the rails in the Wild West, demonstrated that women could thrive in even the harshest environments, proving that the spirit of adventure knows no bounds.

Steam Train Maury, a trailblazer in the 20th century, shattered stereotypes and showed that women could excel in traditionally male-dominated fields. Her passion for trains and her unwavering dedication to her craft inspired a new generation of women to pursue their dreams, regardless of societal expectations. Colleen Anderson, escaping the constraints of society, embraced the nomadic lifestyle of train hopping, finding freedom and independence on the rails. Her story resonates with those who yearn to break free from the confines of a conventional life.

Hobo Girl Petula Williams, a modern-day nomad, continues to carry the torch of the women train hoppers who came before her. Her journey embodies the spirit of adventure and the pursuit of personal freedom. These women, along with countless others, have left an indelible mark on history, challenging gender norms and inspiring future generations to live life on their own terms.

12.1.2 Inspiring Future Generations: The Legacy of Women Train Hoppers

The legacy of women train hoppers extends far beyond their individual stories. Their courage, resilience, and determination have inspired countless individuals, both men and women, to embrace a life of adventure and defy societal expectations. By challenging the status quo, these women have shown that it is possible to live a life of freedom and independence, even in the face of adversity.

Their stories have resonated with individuals from all walks of life, encouraging them to question the limitations placed upon them by society. The women train hoppers have become symbols of empowerment, reminding us that we have the power to shape our own destinies and live life on our own terms.

12.1.3 Representation and Visibility: Women's Stories in Popular Culture

The stories of women train hoppers have not only inspired individuals but have also gained recognition in popular culture. Books, movies, and documentaries have shed light on the lives of these remarkable women, ensuring that their stories are not forgotten. By bringing their experiences to a wider audience, these works of art have helped to challenge stereotypes and broaden our understanding of what it means to be a woman.

Through these mediums, the voices of women train hoppers have been amplified, allowing their stories to reach a global audience. Their tales of adventure, resilience, and self-discovery have captivated the imaginations of people around the world, inspiring them to embrace their own sense of wanderlust and pursue their dreams.

12.1.4 Changing Perspectives: Society's Evolving Attitudes towards Train Hopping

The stories of women train hoppers have played a significant role in changing societal attitudes towards train hopping. Once seen as a predominantly male activity, train hopping is now recognized as a pursuit that knows no gender boundaries. The courage and resilience displayed by women train hoppers have shattered stereotypes and challenged the notion that certain lifestyles are reserved for men.

As society continues to evolve, so too does our understanding of what it means to live a fulfilling life. The stories of women train hoppers have contributed to this evolution, reminding us that true happiness lies in following our passions and embracing the unknown. These women have shown us that it is possible to live a life of adventure, even in a world that often seeks to confine us to predetermined roles and expectations.

12.2 Lessons for Life: What We Can Learn from Their Stories

The stories of women train hoppers offer valuable lessons that can be applied to our own lives. Their journeys teach us the importance of embracing our passions, challenging societal norms, and pursuing our dreams, no matter how unconventional they may seem. By following in the footsteps of these remarkable women, we can find the courage to break free from the limitations that society often places upon us.

Their stories also remind us of the power of resilience and determination. Despite facing numerous challenges and obstacles, these women never gave up. They persevered in the face of adversity, demonstrating that with unwavering determination, we can overcome any obstacle that stands in our way.

Furthermore, the stories of women train hoppers highlight the importance of community and connection. These women formed bonds with fellow train hoppers, creating a supportive network that provided them with a sense of belonging and camaraderie. Their experiences teach us the value of building meaningful connections with others and the strength that can be found in shared experiences.

12.3 The Enduring Spirit of Adventure: Inspiring Others to Follow Their Dreams

The enduring spirit of adventure embodied by women train hoppers continues to inspire individuals around the world. Their stories serve as a reminder that life is meant to be lived to the fullest, and that true fulfillment comes from embracing the unknown and stepping outside of our comfort zones.

By sharing their stories, we hope to inspire others to follow their dreams, no matter how unconventional they may seem. The women train hoppers have shown us that it is possible to live a life of adventure, even in a world that often seeks to confine us to predetermined roles and expectations. Their journeys remind us that the pursuit of happiness and personal fulfillment knows no boundaries.

12.4 Final Thoughts: The Legacy of Women Who Train Hop

As we conclude this book, we are left with a deep appreciation for the women who have chosen to live a life of adventure and defy societal norms. Their stories have left an indelible mark on history, challenging gender roles, inspiring future generations, and changing societal attitudes towards train hopping.

The impact of women train hoppers extends far beyond their individual stories. They have become symbols of empowerment, reminding us that we have the power to shape our own destinies and live life on our own terms. Their stories have inspired individuals around the world to embrace a life of adventure, challenge societal expectations, and pursue their dreams.

The legacy of women train hoppers will continue to inspire

future generations, encouraging them to question the limitations placed upon them by society and embrace a life of freedom and independence. Their stories serve as a reminder that true fulfillment comes from following our passions, challenging the status quo, and embracing the unknown.

As we look back on the impact of women train hoppers, we are reminded of the enduring spirit of adventure that resides within each of us. Their stories serve as a call to action, urging us to embrace our own sense of wanderlust and pursue our dreams, no matter how unconventional they may seem. In doing so, we honor the legacy of these remarkable women and ensure that their stories continue to inspire and empower future generations.

Afterword

Riding the rails is extremely dangerous. Whilst this book lists those women who were forced due to circumstances to ride the rails during times of poverty and hardship, this book does not advocate for women and girls to embrace this culture of train hopping.